*From the Low Tide of the Sea
to the Highest Mountain Tops*

From time immemorial it was the custom and the law of Scotland that, when a new owner was given possession of land, this would be done in a ceremony held on the land itself. In this ceremony, in the presence of witnesses, stone and earth of that land would be handed to the new owner. This ceremony was known as giving sasine. An account of the ceremony was written down in Latin and that account recorded in a Register of Sasines. Through time the recording of the written account became more important, and eventually the ceremony of sasine was abolished. However, it was revived in Gigha last year and we are now going to bring it back to the Western Isles ... I hereby deliver into your hands stone and earth of this land, and in so doing give unto the North Harris Trust true and lawful sasine of these whole lands of North Harris, from the low tide of the sea to the highest mountain tops, *a coelo usque ad centrum*, to be held on behalf of the people of North Harris in all time coming.

Simon Fraser, solicitor, Stornoway, speaking at the formal hand-over of the North Harris Estate to the North Harris Trust, March 2003.

From the Low Tide of the Sea to the Highest Mountain Tops

COMMUNITY OWNERSHIP OF LAND IN THE HIGHLANDS AND ISLANDS OF SCOTLAND

JAMES HUNTER

THE ISLANDS BOOK TRUST

Published in 2012 by The Islands Book Trust

www.theislandsbooktrust.com

Copyright of text: Carnegie UK Trust
Copyright of photographs: Carnegie UK Trust (apart from photographs of Scalpay, Hallaig, Neist Point, Raasay, and Staffin, which are copyright of Cailean Maclean)

ISBN: 978-1-907443-28-2

We gratefully acknowledge financial support from the Carnegie UK Trust

The Islands Book Trust
Ravenspoint
Kershader
Isle of Lewis
HS2 9QA
Tel: 01851 880737

Typeset by Erica Schwarz
Printed and bound by Martins the Printers, Berwick upon Tweed
Cover design by James Hutcheson

Price £15

Contents

Acknowledgements vii

Foreword ix

Map: Present and Prospective Community Land Ownership Groups referred to in the Book xi

CHAPTER 1
Small island, Big Society 1

CHAPTER 2
The people do not own the land 21

CHAPTER 3
We have won the land 45

CHAPTER 4
We just want to buy a little security 81

CHAPTER 5
At last we could force the pace 121

CHAPTER 6
A story not yet ended 169

Perspective 191

Sources and bibliography 195

Index 201

By the same author:

The Making of the Crofting Community

Skye: The Island

For the People's Cause: From the Writings of John Murdoch

The Claim of Crofting

Scottish Highlanders: A People and their Place

A Dance Called America: The Scottish Highlands, the United States and Canada

On the Other Side of Sorrow: Nature and People in the Scottish Highlands

Glencoe and the Indians

Last of the Free: A History of the Highlands and Islands

Culloden and the Last Clansman

Scottish Exodus: Travels among a Worldwide Clan

Acknowledgements

This book would not have been written but for the Carnegie UK Trust having asked me in 2010 to compile a report about community land ownership in the Highlands and Islands. I was then director of the Centre for History at the University of the Highlands and Islands (UHI). The Carnegie UK Trust made funding available to UHI for this purpose – the trust's funding being supplemented by a grant to UHI from Highlands and Islands Enterprise (HIE). I am very grateful to the Carnegie UK Trust and to Highlands and Islands Enterprise for their support. This funding paid for some of my time and covered travel and other research expenses. Both before and after retiring from UHI in May 2011, however, I took it on myself to do rather more research, and write at greater length, than had been envisaged originally. This is because the story this book tells has not been told before and because it seemed to me, and to many people in the community ownership movement, that the story is worth telling.

The resulting book is not, and was not meant to be, a detailed analysis of community land ownership in the Highlands and Islands. This is simply an outline history of how such ownership has come about. The interpretations I place on events, and the opinions I express about them, are mine and mine alone. I am entirely responsible too for any errors of fact the book may contain.

I am grateful to Cailean Maclean, who took the photographs that appear on following pages – photographs that help bring to life both people and places.

Martyn Evans, Douglas White, Jennifer Wallace, Geoff Brown, Kirsty Tait and Nick Wilding at the Carnegie UK Trust have been supportive from the outset. So have John Watt, Sandra Holmes and Liz Howard at HIE – John, Sandra and Liz having also been key sources of information. In addition, my thanks are due to David Ross, Highland correspondent of *The Herald*, who made available to me a number of his own contributions to the community ownership story.

Most of all, however, I am indebted to the many people in the community ownership movement – right across the Highlands and Islands – who have helped and encouraged this venture. They are all busy, and there must have been times when they could have done without my persistent questioning. But they concealed this very well.

Most of those people, though not all, are mentioned by name in my text. But whether they are mentioned or not, I am much obliged to them.

I am also grateful for the chance this project has given me to renew my acquaintance with places I had not visited for some time. Long ago, when working for the Scottish Crofters Union, I happened to remark to a crofter – at a union branch meeting in Ardnamurchan – that my job involved a lot of travelling and that, in consequence, I had seen a great deal of the Highlands and Islands during the preceding four or five years. 'Well,' this crofter replied, 'one thing to be said for our part of the world is that nobody was ever the worse for having the chance to look at it.' That was true then. It still is.

Foreword

This is the remarkable story of community land ownership in Scotland. It deserves a wide audience. The Carnegie UK Trust wanted this book to celebrate what has already been accomplished, and to inspire others to similar and even greater achievements in the future. The message of confidence and trust in the hard work, sense of fairness and inclusiveness of local communities has significance far beyond Scotland and the UK.

James Hunter tells this story with great authority, and in vivid detail, illustrated by the beautiful photographs of Cailean Maclean.

The idea of local communities taking control of their own land and assets should no longer be considered remarkable. It is becoming a normal way of doing things. Rural community land ownership has a mirror in the longer established community based housing associations and housing co-operatives of urban Scotland.

Yet there still remains a sense of unease amongst some about trusting local people and their communities. One of the main purposes of this book is to recall the truly extraordinary individuals who have been responsible for showing that a community can seize control of its own destiny and transform it in a way which few could have imagined. The skill, commitment and resolve of those involved are difficult to overstate. They have shown great fortitude in the face of what must have often appeared to be insurmountable challenges. They have found the confidence to begin; have overcome daunting financial and legal hurdles to make it happen; are now making it work – not just for a day, a week, or a month, but year after year.

The results have been hugely impressive – half a million acres of land are now in community ownership in Scotland, resulting in repopulation; new homes; new businesses; and the unleashing of a new sense of confidence, energy and opportunity.

In many ways this is a story which is only just beginning. Given the right support, these communities can go on to achieve even greater things – and many more communities can join them in enjoying the benefits that owning and controlling local assets, including land, can offer.

Community land and asset ownership will become the story of the 21st century and Scotland's people – and politicians – deserve a reputation of pioneers and successful pathfinders in this hugely rewarding adventure.

Melanie Leech
Chair
Carnegie UK Trust

Martyn Evans
Chief Executive
Carnegie UK Trust

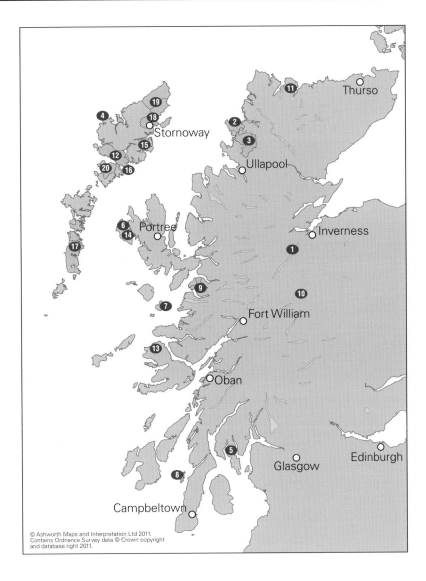

Present and Prospective Community Land Ownership Groups referred to in the Book

Extent of land ownership
(where map scale permits)

1. Abriachan Forest Trust
2. Assynt Crofters Trust
3. Assynt Foundation
4. Bhaltos Community Trust
5. Bute Community Land Company
6. Glendale Estate
7. Isle of Eigg Heritage Trust
8. Isle of Gigha Heritage Trust
9. Knoydart Foundation
10. Laggan Forest Trust
11. Melness Crofters Estate
12. North Harris Trust
13. North West Mull Community Woodland Company
14. Orbost Estate
15. Pairc Trust
16. Scalpay Community Steering Group
17. Stòras Uibhist
18. Stornoway Trust
19. Urras Oighreachd Ghabhsainn
20. West Harris Trust

Thurso

Stornoway

Ullapool

Inverness

Portree

Fort William

Oban

Glasgow

Edinburgh

Campbeltown

Gigha and the Argyll mainland. Many of the homes in the foreground have been built or refurbished because of the island having come into community ownership in 2002.

I

Small island, Big Society

Isle of Gigha Heritage Trust
Localism and the Big Society
Community Land Scotland
Scalpay Community Steering Group

Susan Allan (foreground), who chairs the Isle of Gigha Heritage Trust, meets with colleagues. They are (left to right), Helen McBrearty, Hannah Storrie, John Martin and Neil Bannatyne.

CREIDEAS
DÒCHAS
CARTHANNAS

Gigha Renewable

CHAPTER ONE

Small island, Big Society

Isle of Gigha Heritage Trust § Localism and the Big Society
Community Land Scotland § Scalpay Community Steering Group

Communities buy the land they live on because they see land as the foundation on which all other developments sit. Ownership leads directly to the development of: private enterprise, investment due to security of tenure, affordable housing for rent and purchase, renewable energy schemes and infrastructure development, as well as ongoing estate management. This combination supports increased population and school numbers. The emphasis is on long-term stewardship, investment and growth. Community land trusts are primarily volunteer run … Boards are made up of entirely local, or a combination of local and external, people.

Sarah Skerratt, **Community Land Ownership and Community Resilience: Rural Policy Centre Research Report**, *Scottish Agricultural College, June 2011.*

When Susan Cresswell, then 23, first came to Gigha from Wales in the 1960s to take a job as a gardener with the island's then owner, Sir James Horlick, she intended, she says, to stay for no more than two years. These plans changed when, on Gigha, Susan met and married Malcolm Allan, a member of a local farming family. Some forty-five years after her arrival, Susan Allan, now widowed and retired, still lives in Gigha where, on a sunny morning in mid-February 2011, her continuing commitment to gardening is evident in the brightly flowering crocuses at her front door. 'Spring comes early to Gigha,' Susan comments of this most southerly of the many islands making up the Hebrides. But spring sunshine notwithstanding, Susan, this morning as most mornings, is to be found not in her garden but in the sitting-room that doubles as her office. There framed photographs of Susan's late husband, her sons and her grandchildren take up a lot of shelf space. And there, seated by the computer and associated gadgetry occupying one corner, Susan Allan deals with the emails and other documentation reaching her daily, often hourly or more often, in her capacity as chair of the Isle of Gigha Heritage Trust.

If you knew nothing of Gigha, and were told only that this small island is inhabited by just 150 or so people, you might wonder why chairing the Isle of Gigha Heritage Trust takes up so much of Susan Allan's time. An organisation with *heritage trust* in its title, you might guess, would have a limited role in such a locality. It might concern itself with the history and traditions of the place. It might run a little museum, a visitor centre of some kind; the sort of facility that opens for an hour or two each afternoon in summer when tourists are most likely to come calling. But in so speculating, you would be wrong. Just how wrong is evident from the nature of the agenda confronting Susan Allan and other trust directors when they gather in the Heritage Trust's headquarters for one of the meetings – starting at seven p.m. and lasting until well after ten –

that, despite efforts to reduce trust workloads, commonly require their presence for a minimum of one evening out of seven.

The islanders who sit on the Isle of Gigha Heritage Trust's board have been elected by fellow residents, and they are a cross-section of Gigha's population. John Martin, the heritage trust's vice-chairman, is a joiner who, though nominally retired, still does a lot of joinering. Neil Bannatyne manages a fish farm. Helen McBrearty is, as Susan Allan once was, a gardener by profession. Hannah Storrie is a hotel worker. Ken Abernethy, not an island resident, was co-opted on to the heritage trust board by its elected members. Ken lives on the nearby mainland of Argyll where, prior to his retirement, he was in charge of a development agency. Tonight, as is often the case at trust meetings, his background in finance will come in useful; for among the items scheduled for discussion is a project which, if were to go ahead, would involve the trust in bank borrowings well in excess of £1 million. The financial forecasts accompanying this agenda item – concerning the planned construction of a grid-connected wind turbine – extend many years into the future and consist of column after column of expenditure and income projections. But neither Susan Allan nor her colleagues are in any way unsettled by the figuring in front of them. The Isle of Gigha Heritage Trust, after all, already owns a three-turbine-strong wind farm, to say nothing of a hotel, holiday apartments, a quarry, more than forty homes, business premises, farms, woodland and numerous other assets. While very definitely a community venture, then, the Isle of Gigha Heritage Trust is also a substantial – and successful – business. It has been so since the day in March 2002 when Gigha's residents became the collective owners of their island.

I've never regretted that, on the day the gauntlet of ownership was thrown down in front of us, we had the courage to pick it up … If someone had said nine years ago that we'd have achieved by now as much as we have achieved, I'd have said they were dreaming … What has been realised here on Gigha is far beyond my expectation.

John Martin, vice-chair, Isle of Gigha Heritage Trust, in conversation with the author, 10 February 2011.

The most southerly, and one of the most beautiful, of the Hebridean islands, Gigha is situated three miles west of the Kintyre peninsula [in Argyll] … Gigha is breathtaking – sandy beaches, clear green seas, a host of wildlife … Since the community buy-out in 2002 the island has gone from strength to strength with a growing population that is sustainably developing its local economy. Wind turbines that generate income for the local economy, a housing refurbishment programme that is providing high-quality accommodation for residents, increasing local business activity and a forward-looking trust with directors elected from the island leading the way: Gigha really is moving forward.

Isle of Gigha Heritage Trust website, February 2011.

There are things you do [in government] because it's your duty … But there are things you do because it's your passion. The things that fire you up in the morning, that drive you, that you truly believe will make a real difference to the country you love. And my great passion is the Big Society … The Big Society is about a huge cultural change, where people in their everyday lives, in their homes, in their neighbourhoods, in their workplaces, don't always turn to officials, local authorities or central government for answers to the problems they face, but instead feel both free and powerful enough to help themselves and their own communities … We need to create communities who are in charge of their own destiny, who feel if they club together and get involved they can shape the world around them.

Prime Minister David Cameron, speaking in Liverpool, 19 July 2010.

As it happens, a decision on whether or not to proceed with the Isle of Gigha Heritage Trust's fourth wind turbine is, after some debate, put on hold. This is because of the UK government having made known, hours prior to the trust board's meeting, that ministers are to review the feed-in tariff regime which lays down the price paid for electricity supplied to Britain's national grid from smaller-scale renewable energy sources such as – or so heritage trust directors suspect – Gigha's planned turbine. The government's announcement, then, has the effect of throwing into doubt, for the moment at least, the income assumptions underpinning the financial arrangements heritage trust representatives have been negotiating with a major bank. While it is not impossible that the tariff review will lead to the heritage trust doing better financially than envisaged, trust directors are of the view that – given the wider cost-cutting environment prevailing in 2011 – this is unlikely. In these circumstances, they agree, it would be prudent to pause until the feed-in tariff position clarifies.

Inevitably, there is grumbling about the difficulty thus placed in the way of the Isle of Gigha Heritage Trust's latest initiative. And if any trust directors managed to catch a late-night news bulletin when they got home, they would have detected a certain irony in the timing of the feed-in tariff review announcement. For looming much larger than that announcement on this February evening's television news are the efforts of the United Kingdom's prime minister, David Cameron, to convince the British public that he means what he says when he talks about the urgent need for the country to turn its back on big government and to put its faith instead in what the prime minister calls a Big Society. What is meant exactly by the concept of a Big Society is a matter of some debate in the Britain of 2011. But Susan Allan, John Martin and other directors of the Isle of Gigha Heritage Trust are surely right to believe that their objectives for Gigha and its residents have something in common with what David Cameron has in mind when he speaks about it being his 'passion' to create communities 'in charge of their own destiny'. This being so, the heritage trust's directors are understandably of the opinion that a government wishing to assist endeavours like their's might try a bit harder to ensure that its other policies, such as those having to do with feed-in tariffs, do not get in the way – as the tariff review has done in Gigha's case – of community-based enterprise.

The Big Society is what happens whenever people work together for the common good. It is about achieving our collective goals in ways that are more diverse, more local and more personal … We need to … empower communities to do things their way – by creating rights for people to get involved with, and direct, the development of their communities.

Department for Communities and Local Government, **Decentralisation and the Localism Bill: An Essential Guide,** *December 2010.*

There is nothing intrinsically wrong with David Cameron's idea of the Big Society, except the implication that he had somehow freshly minted the idea himself. Many of Scotland's more remote rural communities, with few public services, would never have survived without local residents prepared to go the extra mile for each other. This brand of community spirit is exemplified by Scotland's … community land trusts, which now own … half a million acres of land between them … [Their] margins of success may vary, but the main lesson learned to date is that this is a process that tends to generate a virtuous circle: new jobs, justifying the construction of affordable housing that attracts new families, sustaining rural schools.

Herald *editorial, 1 July 2011.*

———

The notion that people are entitled to a stake in the land on which they live is not a new one in the Highlands and Islands of Scotland where such thinking has been common for hundreds of years. In more recent centuries, to be sure, ownership has mostly been vested in individuals – a very small number of whom have possessed the bulk of the available acreage. But this state of affairs has never been unquestioned. While historians argue about exactly who was ultimately in control of the land occupied in the middle ages by the region's often quarrelling clans, there continues to be in the Highlands and Islands a widespread belief that not just clan chiefs but the generality of clansfolk had rights in this land – a conviction, as will be seen, given legislative effect towards the end of the nineteenth century. This is emphatically not to contend that present-day community ownership initiatives like Gigha's owe their existence to modes of thought originating in clanship's long-gone heyday. It is to suggest, however, that many residents of the Highlands and Islands have for a long time been out of sympathy with the idea that it is perfectly acceptable for a single individual to be in sole charge of a piece of territory which is home to lots of other people.

A few of the hundreds of thousands of acres brought into community ownership in the Highlands and Islands since 1992.

Feeling of this sort helps buttress support for community ownership in Gigha and in those other parts of the Highlands and Islands where it has taken hold. That helps explain why, in this author's opinion at any rate, the community ownership movement in today's Highlands and Islands cannot be understood without reference to the region's past. But neither should the movement, despite its being rooted in what has gone before in the northern half of Scotland, be considered in isolation from attempts presently being made more widely to nurture, promote and assist community activism of the Gigha variety. 'The Big Society,' according to a UK government publication of December 2010, 'is what happens whenever people work together for the common good.' On that basis, Gigha is the Big Society exemplified. Before returning to the more local origins of what has been happening of late in Gigha and in the other parts of the Highlands and Islands now owned by their residents, then, there is merit in exploring the connection between developments in these places and statements such as this: 'We share a conviction that … centralisation and top-down control have proved a failure and that the time has come to disperse power more widely.'

These words are extracted from the foreword contributed jointly by Conservative leader David Cameron and Liberal Democrat leader Nick Clegg to the published version of the agreement underpinning the coalition government established by the two men and their parties following the UK general election of May 2010. The extent to which power will actually be dispersed as promised remains to be seen – but, in asserting that it ought to be, Clegg and Cameron were aligning themselves with, if not a consensus viewpoint, then with an increasingly influential strand of political thinking. This thinking, as expounded by people like Phillip Blond of the ResPublica thinktank or Julian Le Grand of the London School of Economics, is not easily categorised in conventional left-right terms – something underlined by the title of Blond's 2010 book, *Red Tory*. Governments of the all-controlling type that evolved in Britain during the twentieth century are considered by Le Grand and Blond to be incapable of solving twenty-first century problems. But for all that it is possible to take the view that policy prescriptions of the sort offered by Blond and Le Grand are intended merely to give an intellectual gloss to what would otherwise be barefaced attempts to pave the way for free-market alternatives to state provision in areas like healthcare and education,

Blond and his ResPublica colleagues in particular are by no means sold on the much advertised virtues of an unfettered capitalism. Hence the emphasis they place on mutuality and community ownership as means of liberating energies which, Phillip Blond asserts, neither the state nor the market have the capacity to tap. The work of the Isle of Gigha Heritage Trust, then, is very much of a piece with Blond's ideas. This matters: not because Blond's theorising is to be taken as gospel but because it helps show – to reiterate a previous point – why the Isle of Gigha Heritage Trust cannot be dismissed as a local curiosity. As already stressed, and as subsequent chapters will stress further, community trusts such as Gigha's exhibit plenty of features deriving from their having developed in the Highlands and Islands. But these trusts can also be seen as pointing the way to the 're-localised' society and economy Phillip Blond advocates in *Red Tory*. This is of more than academic interest. To think about the community ownership movement in the Highlands and Islands in these terms is to make a case for the movement's re-evaluation by those media and other commentators in Scotland who regard such ownership as having little or nothing to offer in the context of the need, as they see it, to make Scotland less dependent on 'big government' and on the public sector.

Perhaps because the expansion of community ownership in the Highlands and Islands stems partly from longstanding hostility to the ownership of enormous tracts of land by individuals, and because such hostility, from as far back as the French Revolution of the 1790s if not the English Revolution of the 1640s, has also fuelled demands for land reform of the kind favoured by the political left, anti-leftist newspapers and their columnists have been generally dismissive of what has been happening in Gigha and places like it. Overlooking the extent to which land reform in the Highlands and Islands has been brought about – as underlined later – by Conservative administrations, and insisting that all such reform is inescapably leftist in origin and intent, critics of the land reforms introduced by Scottish governments make little distinction between these reforms and those that resulted in collectivisation or nationalisation in places like the Soviet Union or Cuba. As will be seen in a later chapter, legislation meant to assist organisations like the Isle of Gigha Heritage Trust has consequently been attacked by some Conservative politicians and by their media allies as statist, Marxist, even

There are only two powers in our country: the state and the marketplace. All other sources of independent autonomous power have been crushed. We no longer have, in any effective independent way, local government, churches, trade unions, co-operative societies, publicly funded educational institutions, civic organisations or locally organised groups that operate on the basis of more than single issues. Whatever these various institutions represent now, what they embodied in the past were means for ordinary people to exercise power. These associations helped to give form and direction to human beings; they allowed parents to craft their families and citizens to shape their communities. Nowadays, however, all such sources of independent power have been eroded; instead, these civil spaces have either vanished or become subject-domains of the centralised state or the monopolised market.

Phillip Blond, **Red Tory: How Left and Right Have Broken Britain and How We Can Fix It,** *Faber and Faber, 2010.*

Stalinist. This could be ignored if it were not for the fact that the people putting so much time and effort into community land trusts have themselves come in for media abuse – on the grounds, presumably, that the intended beneficiaries of suspect reforms must be suspect themselves.

Hence the space given here to ideas that have helped inspire Prime Minister Cameron. While the more nonsensical newspaper critiques of what is going on in places such as Gigha are unlikely to survive even the briefest acquaintance with what Susan Allan, John Martin and folk like them are accomplishing, it is nevertheless helpful, courtesy of Phillip Blond and other thinkers of a Tory persuasion, to suggest that the community ownership movement in the Highlands and Islands is not so much a reversion to Soviet-era communism as an attempt to come up with what a recent ResPublica discussion paper calls 'a way of re-endowing communities with independence and self-sufficiency'.

Although his thinking is not always in tune with that of the community land ownership movement, Phillip Blond is particularly relevant in this connection because nowhere is the 'monopolised market' of which he is so condemnatory more absolute than in a land ownership structure of the sort long characteristic of the Highlands and Islands – where, prior to the emergence of the community ownership movement, the overwhelming majority of people were denied any worthwhile say in what happened to the land on which they live. Providing these people with just such a say is arguably to challenge – indeed threaten – the established order much more fundamentally than it is challenged by the generality of the 'social enterprises' which Blond and ResPublica see as integral to any meaningful move in the direction of a Big Society. But there are, all the same, some similarities between the Isle of Gigha Heritage Trust and Britain's hundreds of thousands of locally-based social enterprises – many of them (and in this they are at one with Gigha's heritage trust) every bit as entrepreneurial and development-minded as any conventionally-owned private company.

Cliff Prior, chief executive officer of UnLtd, a charity set up to support social entrepreneurs, describes such entrepreneurs on the homepage of UnLtd's website as

---

The state needs to redefine its relationship with individuals and, crucially, with communities. It must find a way of re-endowing communities with independence and self-sufficiency, of giving them the wherewithal to transform themselves and their neighbourhoods.

Steve Wyler and Phillip Blond, **To Buy, To Bid, To Build: Community Rights for an Asset-Owning Democracy,** *ResPublica, 2010.*

There are 1.7 million social ventures overall in the UK, some 62,000 of which are social enterprises, which contribute £24 billion to the economy and employ at least 800,000 people. These enterprises are ambitious, and are as capital-hungry as small businesses: one-third of social enterprises have sought finance over the past 12 months, while 60 per cent of all funding required by social enterprise is expansionary investment for new projects or service development.

Phillip Blond, **The Venture Society,** *ResPublica, May 2010.*

'people with vision, drive, commitment and passion who want to change the world for the better.' Prior's words apply every bit as much to individuals involved in community land ownership in the Highlands and Islands as they do to their numerous counterparts who are presently organising and managing a huge variety of businesses, services and community facilities in practically every corner of the United Kingdom.

Social enterprises need not own physical assets. But many do. In this category are England's growing number of community land trusts. Unlike the Isle of Gigha Heritage Trust and its counterparts in the Highlands and Islands, these bodies own small acreages and, also unlike Gigha's heritage trust, they mostly concentrate on a single area of activity – usually having to do with the provision of affordable housing in rural localities where such housing is extremely hard to come by. However, the underlying structure of community land trusts in places like Cornwall and Cumbria's Eden District – selected as a Big Society 'vanguard area' by the UK government – is in some ways similar to that of community ownership trusts in the Highlands and Islands. Both sets of organisations are run on a voluntary basis by the same sort of people – people whose aim is to renew and revitalise the places where they live. Interestingly, however, England's community land trusts attract none of the rancorous comments that elements of the political right make about their Highlands and Islands equivalents. Indeed quite the reverse. In 2008 the Conservative Party established a Community Land Trust Taskforce with the remit of finding out what needs to be done to make it easier for such trusts to be set up. This commitment to helping the community land trust sector has been carried into government by the Conservative-Liberal Democrat

UnLtd is the foundation for social entrepreneurs in the UK. In our eight years of work, we have supported thousands of people to start up new social ventures. Their commitment, energy and innovation are truly remarkable … Social and community entrepreneurs are not a creation of any government or political group: they are motivated by their own passion to improve the world in which they live … They are a genuine movement.

Cliff Prior, 'Preface', The Venture Society, ResPublica, May 2010.

Social entrepreneurship is an area of rapid and sustained growth … As such, it is important to understand more about what social entrepreneurship can do, socially, environmentally and politically. UnLtd's mission is to reach out and unleash the energies of those individuals who can transform the world in which they live; supporting individuals who have passion, ideas and a can-do attitude to set up and run a social venture. Whether the problem they tackle is local or societal, UnLtd sees this potential for social change in ordinary people with practical solutions.

UnLtd, Social Entrepreneurs: The Facts, March 2010.

Community Land Trusts are established in communities to acquire assets and then to hold them in perpetuity for local use. They work on a non-profit basis, raising money from new sources and unlocking existing resources, to provide housing … and other accommodation. They work on the basis that occupiers pay for the use of buildings and services at prices they can afford, while the value of land, subsidies, planning gain and other equity benefits are locked up on behalf of the wider community – in order to keep affordable housing available in perpetuity.

Geoff Brown, **The Community Land Trust Story in Rural England and Wales,** *Carnegie UK Trust, May 2011.*

coalition – the sector expecting to be a beneficiary of the government's Big Society agenda. That such expectations are well founded was borne out in August 2011 when Prime Minister David Cameron was persuaded to visit Eden District by the locality's Conservative MP, Rory Stewart, a prominent exponent of the virtues of community land trusts – Stewart seizing the opportunity, as he put it in his blog, to show the prime minister some 'tangible results of strong community action'.

Also in the asset-owning business, though usually operating on a smaller scale than community land trusts, are those other social enterprises which have come into existence with a view to their taking over, for the benefit of particular localities, facilities such as shops, post-offices, libraries, parks or redundant school buildings. Typical of many such ventures is the George and Dragon pub in the Yorkshire village of Hudswell. When the pub was put up for sale, with the probable result that it would be closed and converted into a holiday home, the George and Dragon – after a period of frenzied fund-raising – was acquired by a local voluntary grouping set up for this purpose, and in its new guise opened in June 2010. Today pub sales of food and drink are above anticipated levels, ten community allotments have been established in the pub's grounds, and the pub, as well as providing meeting spaces, is hosting a library and a village shop.

Rock is a picturesque village situated in the parish of St Minver Lowlands on the Camel Estuary in North Cornwall. In North Cornwall it takes sixteen times average household income to buy a house of average value and in Rock the figure is much higher. It is reputedly one of the most expensive places in the world to purchase a home, with high levels of second home ownership and holiday lets, making it virtually impossible for first time buyers to access the market … In December 2008 St Minver Community Land Trust completed twelve two and three bedroom self-build affordable sale homes for local people, sold at 33 per cent of open market value … A second phase started on site during March 2010. This … will provide four homes for social rent … and eight self-build plots.

National Community Land Trust website, August 2011.

It was an enormous honour to welcome the Prime Minister to Crosby Ravensworth and to introduce him to some of the key local community members, who have made such incredible progress in the Big Society vanguard right here in the Eden Valley. The Prime Minister was

The Outer Hebrides in summer.

obviously impressed by what he saw and heard. It's wonderful to have had the opportunity to show him the tangible results of strong community action, and what it can achieve. He has seen how Cumbria and its rural communities are the true model of volunteerism, and how community aspirations can succeed against the odds.

Rory Stewart MP, (Conservative: Penrith and the Borders), website, August 2011.

It has been a memorable thirteen months in which we have travelled from a hopeful proposal launched in the depths of winter to become the first community co-op pub in Yorkshire … opened on a balmy day in June [by local Conservative MP and Foreign Secretary William Hague]. The pub is now a thriving business, and has ten community allotments, a library, free internet access and a village shop – all run from the George and Dragon.

Hudswell Community Pub Ltd., Annual Report, February 2011.

While community-owned pubs – whether Hudswell's George and Dragon or the public bar in Gigha's hotel – are still comparatively rare, community-owned shops are becoming numerous. Although the Highlands and Islands helped pioneer the concept of the community-owned store as long ago as the 1970s, initiatives of this kind are now more common in rural England where the Plunkett Foundation, established at the start of the twentieth century to promote the development of agricultural co-operatives, has found a new and welcome *raison d'être* as a source of help and advice to the many communities looking to take over village shops that would otherwise go under.

The hardest step to take, as any self-help manual begins by explaining, is the first. Organisations that are geared to making that step less formidable are invaluable. One of the foremost is the Plunkett Foundation, which has become the engine of the burgeoning rural community shop and pub sector. The foundation is a second flowering of an idea that came from a visionary Anglo-Irishman, Horace Plunkett, who, in the late nineteenth century, saw the co-operative movement as a way of bringing some security to struggling dairy farmers in the Irish south-west. As the political situation worsened, he persevered in reforming the administration of Irish agriculture and, when Dublin became too hostile an environment (he was a moderate nationalist at a time when moderation was out of fashion), he took his ideas … to England. His Plunkett Foundation tottered on for another fifty years … until it found a new mission, once again among struggling rural communities where … pubs and shops … were under attack from the cheap convenience of out-of-town supermarkets. The foundation is now the essential first call for any community that wants to keep a shop or pub going. It provides, mostly for free, retail expertise, advice and guides … It is the co-operators' co-operative.

Guardian, *20 June 2011.*

The sheer scale of the Isle of Gigha Heritage Trust's operations indubitably differentiates the trust from organisations in charge of single businesses. But any Gigha listener to *The Archers*, the 'everyday story of country folk' that is BBC Radio 4's longest-running series, will nevertheless be all too familiar with the tensions and conflicts which emerge when the fictional Ambridge's village shop – in a storyline based on a real-life initiative in the Gloucestershire village of Almondsbury – goes into community ownership. In the case of Gigha, where not just a single business but almost all of an island and most of its assets are owned in this way, such tensions and conflicts are liable to be still more acute. How to strike the right balance between the wider community's expectation of openness and heritage trust directors' need to maintain, on occasion, commercial confidence? How to reconcile differing views as to the best way forward? How to counter the suspicion, which can easily arise, that trust directors are in some way using, or abusing, their positions to advance personal agendas, even personal financial interests? How to find employees who combine necessary managerial skills with an ability to get on with the wider community to whom they are ultimately responsible? These and other problems can become so wearing – especially when the initial excitement of ownership has waned – as to produce volunteer fatigue, even volunteer burn-out.

It is easy for a community to unite in criticising a distant … private landowner. It is relatively easy to make common cause in campaigning for community ownership. But it is far more difficult to sustain the commitment and high levels of participation after the first flush of enthusiasm has worn off. It can prove hard, too, to maintain the initial unity when faced with practical management dilemmas, conflicting visions and the shared responsibilities of ownership.

Charles Warren, Managing Scotland's Environment, *Edinburgh University Press, 2009.*

The number of communities clubbing together to save village shops has soared since radio soap opera, *The Archers*, featured attempts by the residents of Ambridge to take over their threatened shop … Vanessa Whitburn, editor of *The Archers*, said: 'Like many *Archers* stories, the community shop storyline operates on different levels. For listeners interested in how they might save their own village shop, there's information on setting up the necessary committees, securing support from volunteers, and ways of fundraising. For those who love good drama, there's angst for Susan [who's long worked in the shop] as she faces losing her job at a time of recession, conflict between [activist] Pat and [businessman] Brian as they debate whether community or profit should prevail, and warmth as a village pulls together to save one of its precious assets.

guardian.co.uk, *30 December 2009.*

One way of dealing with such difficulties is to get together with others who are also experiencing them. Hence the involvement of the Carnegie UK Trust, a charity that aims to influence public policy and to back innovative social action, in efforts to foster links between England's community land trusts and analogous organisations in the Highlands and Islands. Hence, too, the emergence of Community Land Scotland, an umbrella body comprising twenty or so local groups which, like the Isle of Gigha Heritage Trust, own substantial tracts of land and which, again like the Isle of Gigha Heritage Trust, are endeavouring to develop a range of commercial and other activities on that land.

———————

John Martin of the Isle of Gigha Heritage Trust with a trust-owned boat which he took the lead in constructing. The boat's Gaelic name, Saorsa, *means Freedom.*

Community Land Scotland's first annual conference takes place in Harris over two days at the end of March 2011, and more than seventy people are here. Some are drawn from Community Land Scotland membership organisations which, between them, own around 500,000 acres – an area roughly equivalent to that of an English county like Nottinghamshire, West Yorkshire or West Sussex. Others belong to community groups which, though not owning land, either aspire to do so or are interested in hearing about the benefits, and costs, of such ownership. Although Community Land Scotland, as its name suggests, aims eventually to operate on an all-Scotland basis, most of the people attending its initial gathering are from Highlands and Islands localities. They represent, for example, Sleat Community Trust, North West Mull Community Woodland Company, the Assynt Foundation, the Stornoway Trust, Stòras Uibhist (one of several community ownership groups to have opted for a Gaelic designation), Pairc Trust, Tiree Community Development Trust, Urras Sgire Oighreachd Bharabhaist, North Harris Trust, Helmsdale and District Development Group, Bays of Harris Association, Bhaltos Community Trust, Bute Community Land Company, Borve and Annishader Township, the Knoydart Foundation, Urras Oighreachd Ghabhsainn, West Harris Crofting Trust and Urras Mhangurstaigh.

John Martin is in Harris on behalf of the Isle of Gigha Heritage Trust. The geography of the Highlands and Islands not making for easy travel between the most southerly and one of the more northerly islands in the Hebrides, his getting to Community

Community land trusts identified the importance of Community Land Scotland as an organisation to lobby on their behalf. Although a number of trusts are themselves lobbying and engaging with their local players in different sectors, there was considerable emphasis placed on a voice for the collective, which can engage at strategic, national level with government ... and with significant other non-governmental organisations, development agencies [and] public sector bodies such as local authorities.

Sarah Skerratt, Community Land Ownership and Community Resilience: Rural Policy Centre Research Report, *Scottish Agricultural College, June 2011.*

Much of Harris, where Community Land Scotland held its first annual conference, is today in community ownership.

Community Land Scotland is a new membership organisation … Its aims are:

§ To promote and represent the interests of community landowners across Scotland at all levels of local and national government;

§ To promote the benefits of community landownership and to proactively encourage new landowners;

§ To collaborate with all other relevant membership and support organisations to ensure appropriate support services are provided to community landowners;

§ To facilitate networking and mutual support among community landowners.

Community Land Scotland, Business Plan, June 2010.

Land Scotland's initial gathering has involved a ferry crossing from Gigha to the Argyll mainland, a 100-plus mile drive to Glasgow, a flight from Glasgow to Stornoway on the Isle of Lewis and a further lengthy drive (Lewis and Harris being a single landmass) from Stornoway Airport to the Harris hotel where, over more than twenty-four hours, John and his fellow delegates map out the way ahead for Community Land Scotland. 'It's good to be here,' John says. That is the general feeling. Evaluation feedback from conference attendees reveals a very high degree of satisfaction with proceedings – not least with the several workshops devoted to business expansion, housing provision, financing the land acquisition process and other challenges of the sort that confront, very much on a day to day basis, those Highlands and Islands communities which have become, or which aim to be, owners of the land around them.

Among conference participants is Jenna Cumming. She is a member of Scalpay Community Steering Group – set up, just a couple of weeks prior to the Community Land Scotland conference, as a result of one of the more remarkable developments in the story of how so much land in the Highlands and Islands has gone into community ownership.

Scalpay, smaller than Gigha but with twice Gigha's population, is an island to the east of Harris which, since 1997, has been linked to the Harris mainland by a bridge. Owned by Fred Taylor, a London restaurateur and businessman whose father bought Scalpay in the 1970s, the island was offered by its proprietor to its residents free of charge in February 2011. 'I've spent time looking at how communities have embraced the opportunity of community ownership and seen how it has renovated

§ Lots of new faces and new contacts. Lots of common thinking and vision and lots of good ideas to build on.

§ The best thing I learned was how well other communities are doing and how much they have achieved – an inspiration to pass on.

§ An excellent first conference. More power to the organisers.

§ One of the best and most purposeful events I have been to in a long while.

Feedback comments to Community Land Scotland following its first annual conference, March 2011.

areas,' Scalpay's laird commented in the course of the circular he sent to islanders to tell them of his plan to make them Scalpay's owners. 'My intention,' Fred Taylor continued, 'is that, if the community wish to be involved, then the land [of Scalpay] will be handed over, at no cost, to the benefit of the community.'

At a packed public meeting in Scalpay's small community hall on 9 March 2011, Scalpay's landlord repeated his proposal. 'I really do believe that the transfer of land to community ownership is an obvious way forward for a lot of communities across Scotland,' Fred Taylor said. 'I have to consider future generations, and in my mind there is no question that the way forward is for the people of this island to take [it] over.' Jenna Cumming, well-known on the Gaelic music circuit and, at 26, one of Scalpay's younger residents, was appointed that same evening to the committee given the job of working out how people on Scalpay might most constructively respond to

Scalpay – whose inhabitants were offered their island free of charge by its landlord, Fred Taylor, in 2011.

By 2025, community land ownership will be held up as the best model of sustainable community regeneration and shall be widely supported by government and its agencies through long-term, stable and accessible mechanisms enabling purchase and development.

Community Land Scotland vision statement, June 2010.

Mr Taylor's extraordinarily generous offer. 'I think this is a tremendous opportunity,' she commented. 'I love living on Scalpay and I love the way of life [here] … But there is a definite need for development to attract young people to the island.'

As spring turns to summer on Scalpay, Fred Taylor is working on the house he is building on the tiny offshore island that will be the only bit of his Hebridean estate to remain in his possession. 'Since I became Scalpay's landlord on my father's death in 1998,' he says, 'I've given a lot of thought to what it means to own land. I've become very interested in what's been achieved in those places where communities have taken ownership of land in their vicinity. I find their example inspiring, and I hope very much that something similar can happen in Scalpay. We're now three months into this process and what we're seeing is really exciting. There are boxes here and there where people can leave their suggestions as to what should be thought about, what should be done. There's no lack of ideas. But what exactly takes shape is not for me to say. It's a matter for the community. Over the next year or two, I intend to give up the various roles I have in London and to live here permanently. By then, I'll no longer be Scalpay's owner. The community will be in charge.'

From Fred Taylor's perspective, community ownership of land is bringing into existence what he calls 'a new area of democracy' – one meriting, he believes, the widest possible backing. 'I hope very much that community ownership takes off more and more,' he comments. 'I hope too that the Scottish government helps as much as it can to make this possible.'

Fred Taylor's stance is shared by Community Land Scotland which has the stated aim of having community land ownership 'held up by 2025 as the best model of sustainable community regeneration'. For community ownership of land to be so regarded in the not too distant future would be remarkable. But, as subsequent chapters show, it is equally remarkable how much progress has already been made in this direction.

A Hebridean crofting community of the sort whose survival was guaranteed by the Crofters Act of 1886. This one, Siadar in Lewis, is now in community ownership.

2

THE PEOPLE DO NOT OWN THE LAND

Beginnings of land reform
The Cheviot, the Stag and the Black, Black Oil
Glendale Estate
Stornoway Trust
John McEwen
West Highland Free Press

CHAPTER TWO

The people do not own the land

Beginnings of land reform § *The Cheviot, the Stag and the Black, Black Oil*
Glendale Estate § Stornoway Trust § John McEwen § *West Highland Free Press*

A summer agricultural show in a crofting locality.

Ever since the state-backed transformation of former clan chiefs into commercially-minded landlords was completed in the wake of the failed Jacobite Rebellion of 1745–46, the Highlands and Islands have seldom been free of controversy caused by the use made of the area's land by its owners. Because their power and status derived from the number of fighting men at their command, clan chiefs tended to sustain and nurture population. New-style landlords, whose prestige and position depended on cash income, had different priorities. Their aim was to maximise the revenue-producing potential of their estates. And when, in the years around 1800, it became apparent that there was a lot of money to be made from leasing large parts of those estates to sheep farmers, this was done across the region. Among the consequences were the mass evictions – involving thousands of families – known as the Highland Clearances. Many clearance victims left for North America and Australia. Others, however, remained in the Highlands and Islands. There they were mostly accommodated on coastal smallholdings or crofts. These often amounted to no more than three, four or five acres of indifferent arable land – crofters being expected to supplement their incomes from non-agricultural activities such as fishing.

In the overcrowded crofting townships thus created, poverty was endemic and, since families had no other way of feeding themselves, reliance on potatoes became almost total. The predictable result, when the potato harvest failed repeatedly in the 1840s, was famine – accompanied in many places by renewed clearance and still more emigration.

Eventually, in the early 1880s, the discontents thus engendered found an outlet in riots, rent-strikes and land seizures which, in turn, led to the emergence of the Highland Land League, a protest group sufficiently well organised to have its parliamentary

Lord and Lady Stafford were pleased *humanely* to order a new arrangement of this Country. That the interior should be possessed by Cheviot Shepherds [meaning sheep farmers] and the people brought down to the coast and placed there in lotts [meaning crofts] under the size of three arable acres, sufficient for the maintenance of an industrious family, but pinched enough to cause them turn their attention to the fishing. I presume to say that the proprietors *humanely* ordered this arrangement because it surely was a most benevolent action to put these barbarous hordes into a position where they could better associate together, apply to industry, educate their children and advance in civilization.

Patrick Sellar, factor or land manager on the Highland estate of the Marquis and Marchioness of Stafford, afterwards first Duke and Duchess of Sutherland, May 1815: R. J. Adam (ed), Papers on Sutherland Estate Management, Scottish History Society, 1972.

candidates defeat those of more established parties in several Highlands and Islands constituencies. When repression in the shape of police actions and military deployments failed to restore order, the British government responded to Land League demands with legislation which greatly restricted the powers at the disposal of Highlands and Islands landlords. This legislation, the Crofters Act of 1886, made further clearance impossible both by granting security of tenure to crofters and by making secure tenancies heritable – meaning that a crofter, as well as being personally immune from eviction, could ensure that one of his children, or another family member, succeeded to his croft.

In thus guaranteeing the survival of crofting, the Liberal prime minister of the day, William Gladstone, accepted in effect the longstanding Highlands and Islands contention that, when estate owners of the modern type took the place of clan chieftains, crofters had in effect been robbed of rights – including a right to permanent and undisturbed occupation of land – enjoyed for centuries by their clansfolk forebears.

But for all its acceptance of the Land League case for security of tenure, Gladstone's government was not prepared to countenance the still more far-reaching action required to meet the further Land League demand that the Highland Clearances be reversed by making available to crofters some part of the extensive tracts of territory given over to sheep farms or to the deer forests and other sporting preserves which, by the nineteenth century's close, were beginning to take sheep farming's place.

Ruined homes at Hallaig on the Isle of Raasay. This was one of hundreds of such communities emptied completely of people during the Highland Clearances.

The opinion so often expressed before us that the small tenantry of the Highlands have an inherited and inalienable title to security of tenure in their possessions, while rent and service are duly rendered, is an impression indigenous to the country, though it has never been sanctioned by legal recognition.

Commissioners of Inquiry into the Condition of the Crofters and Cottars in the Highlands and Islands of Scotland, **Report, May 1884.**

For it is, after all, this historical fact that constitutes the crofters' title to demand the interference of parliament. It is not because they are poor, or because there are too many of them, or because they want more land to support their families, but because those whom they represent had rights of which they have been surreptitiously deprived to the injury of the community.

Prime Minister William Gladstone, January 1885: Ewen A. Cameron, **Land for the People: The British Government and the Scottish Highlands, 1880– 1925, Tuckwell Press, 1996.**

Other politicians had none of Gladstone's inhibitions. In 1897, a Conservative administration headed by Lord Salisbury, set up an agency, the Congested Districts Board, empowered – as its title indicates – to ease congestion in crofting townships by taking land into state ownership as a prelude to having it settled by crofters. Further such initiatives followed. They culminated in much the most radical land reform measure (not excluding the Scottish parliament's Land Reform Act of 2003) ever adopted in Britain. Devised and enacted by a Conservative-Liberal coalition government, the last such UK government before the present one, the Land Settlement (Scotland) Act of 1919 empowered the Board (afterwards the Department) of Agriculture for Scotland to acquire still more land for crofting occupation – and to obtain such land, if necessary, by compulsion. When this legislation's outcomes were added to what had already been accomplished, the overall result was the creation, often on land that had been cleared a century or so before, of many hundreds of new crofts.

An abandoned island home. Long after the clearances ended, opportunities were few in many Highlands and Islands localities – with depopulation consequently continuing. This is why job creation is a priority for many of today's community ownership trusts.

At this point, however, reforming impetus faltered. While providing additional crofts was all very well, and while it was certainly in accord with Highlands and Islands opinion, no such effort, especially in an era of falling agricultural prices, could of itself turn round a regional economy characterised by a chronic lack of the employment needed both by crofters – most of them still part-time agriculturalists – and by Highlands and Islands residents more generally. In these circumstances, and against a backdrop of the continuing population outflow made inevitable by a scarcity of jobs, policy concerned itself less and less with land reform and more and more with wider economic development – to be achieved, it was hoped, by agencies like the North of Scotland Hydro Electric Board, set up in 1943, and the Highlands and Islands Development Board (HIDB), launched in 1965.

The fact that so many crofters have the government as their landlord is not … the result of some long-forgotten experiment in socialism. Labour administrations have never been very keen on Highland land reform which … has largely been the prerogative of governments controlled or dominated by Conservatives. Thus it was in 1897, some years before the Labour Party was formed and during the premiership of the impeccably Tory Lord Salisbury, that the [British] cabinet set out on the reforming road that was to culminate in the state acquiring some 800,000 acres for settlement by crofters.

James Hunter, 'The DAFS Crofting Estates: A Case for Community Control', in, John Hulbert (ed), Land: Ownership and Use, Andrew Fletcher Society, 1986.

For two hundred years the Highlander has been the man on Scotland's conscience … No part of Scotland has been given a shabbier deal by history … Too often there has been only one way out of his troubles for the person born in the Highlands: emigration.

Willie Ross, Secretary of State for Scotland, introducing to the House of Commons the legislation which established the Highlands and Islands Development Board, 16 March 1965.

If there is bitterness in my voice, I can assure the House that there is bitterness in Scotland too when we recollect the history of these areas … We have nine million acres, where 225,000 people live, and we are short of land. Surely one of the first powers which must be given is a power related to the proper use of the land itself. To my mind, this is basic to any improvement in the Highlands and Islands. Anyone who denies the [Highlands and Islands Development] Board powers over land is suggesting that the board should not function effectively at all … Land is the basic natural resource of the Highlands and any plan for social and economic development would be meaningless if proper use of the land were not a part of it … Clearly the board must have power to acquire land, by compulsion if necessary, if it is to be effective.

Willie Ross, Secretary of State for Scotland, introducing to the House of Commons the legislation which established the Highlands and Islands Development Board, 16 March 1965.

Harris Tweed manufacture is one of the industries which have flourished in conjunction with crofting.

Despite this policy shift, one constant element can be discerned in the attempts made by successive governments to deal with Highlands and Islands difficulties. When Willie Ross, Secretary of State for Scotland in the Labour government that came to power in 1964, introduced into the House of Commons the following year the legislation which established the HIDB, he followed Gladstone in maintaining that the Highlands and Islands had a particular claim on government for reasons stemming from the region's past ill-treatment. Since this ill-treatment was bound up with the origins of a landholding system that Ross considered a major obstacle in the way of the various improvements the HIDB was meant to bring about, he insisted (in the course of a powerful Commons speech) that the board had to have 'powers over land'. In the event, however, the powers provided were not adequate to the task, and the HIDB, while doing lots of other good things, made no substantial contribution to altering the north of Scotland's land ownership structure. As the board's failings in this regard became increasingly apparent during the early 1970s, demands for something to be done by way of remedying these failings began to be made. One of the most powerful such demands consisted of a dramatic production taken on tour in the Highlands and Islands in 1973 by playwright John McGrath and his 7:84 Theatre Company.

This production, a play with ceilidh-like song and music, was *The Cheviot, the Stag and the Black, Black Oil*. Its core contention, as suggested by its title, was that – whether by clearing landlords, the often absentee owners of sporting estates or the multinational corporations then beginning to take an interest in the north of Scotland's offshore oilfields – people in the Highlands and Islands had been denied jurisdiction over their area's natural resources. Crofters had won substantial victories in the 1880s and in ensuing decades, McGrath and his company agreed. But those victories, they argued, had been incomplete. Hence the insistent message of *The Cheviot*'s concluding scene: 'The people do not own the land. The people do not control the land.' Action was urgently required, or so the play asserted, to alter this state of affairs.

We are the men
Who own your glen,
Though you won't see us there –
In Edinburgh pubs
And Guildford clubs,
We insist how much we care:
Your interests
Are ours, my friends,
From Golspie to the Minch –
But if you want your land,
We'll take a stand,
We will not budge one inch.

John McGrath, The Cheviot, the Stag and the Black, Black Oil, *Eyre Methuen, 1981.*

The theatre can never *cause* a social change. It can articulate the pressures towards one, help people to celebrate their strengths and maybe build their self-confidence. It can be a public emblem of inner, and outer, events, and occasionally a reminder, an elbow-jogger, a perspective-bringer. Above all, it can be the way people can find their voice, their solidarity and their collective determination. If we achieved any one of those, it was enough.

John McGrath, 'The Year of the Cheviot', in, John McGrath, The Cheviot, the Stag and the Black, Black Oil, *Eyre Methuen, 1981.*

If I die tomorrow, I will die a happier man for having seen the story of my people told in this way.

Gaelic poet Murdo MacFarlane, Melbost, Lewis, congratulating John McGrath on the night of The Cheviot's *performance in Stornoway.*

Even in the early 1970s, when *The Cheviot, the Stag and the Black, Black Oil*, was being staged in small towns and villages all over the Highlands and Islands, there was land in what would today be called community ownership. The longest-established instance of such ownership was, and is, to be found in Glendale, a crofting district in the north-western corner of Skye. During the 1880s, the Glendale Estate had been one of the leading centres of crofting protest and there was some symbolic significance, therefore, in its being acquired by the Congested Districts Board in 1904. A Conservative creation answering to a Conservative government, the board was looking to bring about on the Glendale Estate, and on the two or three other Highlands and Islands properties it bought at much the same time, a restructuring of the kind already underway to Ireland. There Conservative governments, at a point when all of Ireland was still a part of the United Kingdom, began to take estate after estate into public ownership with the aim of transferring ownership of this land to its agricultural occupants by

Neist Point, Skye, is part of the Glendale Estate.

means of 50-year purchase agreements. The process thus initiated made Ireland what it has ever since remained, both north and south of the present-day border between Northern Ireland and the Irish Republic, a country of owner-occupying farmers and smallholders. Much the same sort of thing was expected to happen in Glendale and in the other Highlands and Islands localities purchased by the Congested Districts Board. But other than in Glendale, where residents opted to stick with purchase arrangements on the Irish model, crofters showed no great interest in owner-occupation or 'peasant proprietorship' as it was then called. Having had absolute security of tenure since 1886 and fearing (rightly) that ownership would leave them liable to higher local authority rates and other levies, they preferred to remain tenants – in effect, tenants of government.

An identical course was followed by crofters on the much larger areas taken over by the Board of Agriculture for Scotland, the Congested District Board's successor body, in the aftermath of the First World War. In Glendale, however, the 150 or so crofters on the estate were by then on the road to becoming owner-occupiers of their holdings – and, more significantly in the present context, the collective owners of those assets, including areas of farmland and a number of buildings, pertaining to the estate

The [Congested Districts] Board originally thought that the holders of all the estates bought by the board would gladly become purchasing proprietors … This was a complete miscalculation and shows the difference between Ireland, where [individual] ownership is fervidly desired, and the Highlands, where security of tenure and heritability of tenure are clearly seen as the important matters. The Crofters Act of 1886 had given this security and heritability of tenure, so there was no need to buy. Glendale … [contained] the only … communities to decide to become occupying owners.

Frank Fraser Darling, **West Highland Survey,** *Oxford University Press, 1955.*

The purchase price that had to be found by Glendale's crofting families was equivalent to something like £1 million in today's money. This had to come out of Glendale people's own pockets. They got no grants, no help of any kind. In fact, by becoming owner-occupiers, and so ceasing to be crofters in the strictly legal sense of the term, Glendale people actually cut themselves off from a lot of the cash aids that were increasingly available to crofting tenants. And because shares in the estate's collectively-held assets could be retained by people who'd ceased to live here, not all these shares are now in the hands of local residents. Still, the fact that shares can be bought and sold has made it possible for families moving into Glendale to become shareholders. This has meant that a majority of the 150 or so original shares are still owned locally – and there's definitely a strong commitment here to making the best use of those parts of the estate that are in common ownership. The estate farm – on land that had been cleared and which was never brought back into crofting tenure – is operated in ways that provide local employment. The estate's built properties are managed with a view to their generating enough income to cover their maintenance. But things can be difficult. People here are committed to keeping the estate going and they have lots of ideas as to what could be done with it. But because we don't have access to the sort of funding more recent purchasers can get, it's hard to get new ventures going.

Glendale resident Liza Cleland, who has taken a close interest in the locality's twentieth-century history, in correspondence with the author, September 2011.

as a whole rather than to particular crofts. Although community ownership of the assets in question did not become absolute until the last 50-year purchase payments were made in the 1950s, the origins of this ownership are to be found in Glendale people's response – a unique response as it proved – to the opportunity made available to them by the Congested District Board half-a-century before. Hence Glendale's claim to have pioneered, in the Highlands and Islands anyway, the community ownership of land.

If there was something a little bit accidental in Glendale's experiment in community ownership, in that it was a by-product of making the estate's tenants owner-occupiers, this was certainly not true of the second, and rather later, such experiment – this one on a much larger scale – which took place not in Skye but in Lewis. This experiment's origins were bound up with the failure of the various developmental initiatives undertaken by William Hesketh Lever, Lord Leverhulme, who had bought the island in 1918 – just months prior to the end of the First World War. Leverhulme, a soap manufacturer and founder of the transnational corporation known eventually as Unilever, aimed to boost the Lewis economy by providing the island with a fish-canning industry. But with Hebridean fisheries failing to live up to his expectations, his finances weakened by post-war recession and his plans opposed by newly demobilised servicemen who wanted crofts on their landlord's farms, not jobs in his promised factories, Leverhulme, by September 1923, had decided to quit the island. While his obvious way out, he told a meeting he convened that month, would have been to put Lewis up for sale, he had concluded that, rather than do this, he would 'make a gift of the whole of the island' to its residents.

While arguably less generous than it might seem, in that estates of the Lewis sort were then almost unsellable, Leverhulme's gesture was as altruistic as it was unprecedented. Nevertheless, his offer – in part at least – was rejected with the result that community ownership of an entire Hebridean island would not become a reality for another seventy years.

Lord Leverhulme's gift of ownership, if accepted in its totality, would have required two local groups to take possession of Lewis. The first such group, who

I am leaving Lewis with deep regrets. I am carrying with me the happiest recollections of my five years' residence … I hope you will receive my proposals as indicating my desire, when leaving Lewis, to do all in my power to secure the future welfare, prosperity and happiness of its people.

William Hesketh Lever, Lord Leverhulme, September 1923: Roger Hutchinson, The Soapman: Lewis, Harris and Lord Leverhulme, Birlinn, 2003.

were in fact to take what was on offer to them, had the option of taking control of the area around Stornoway, the island's principal population centre and the only town of consequence in the Hebrides. The other, had it taken shape, would have been in charge of the remainder of the island. Especially in the economically parlous circumstances of 1923, when many crofting families in Lewis were so hard-pressed as to be going hungry, few could see how this second – enormously extensive – property could be made financially viable. Croft rents, subject (as they still are) to control by a quasi-judicial body since 1886, were increasingly nominal and were unlikely even to meet annual administrative costs, tax bills and other unavoidable obligations. Nor was there in early twentieth-century Lewis, any more than in Glendale, institutional backing for community ownership of the sort that would emerge towards the century's end. Members of the Lewis District Committee, made up of local authority councillors representing localities beyond the immediate vicinity of Stornoway, were anxious, as they stressed at a meeting with civil servants in September 1923, 'to co-operate in carrying out Lord Leverhulme's public-spirited and generous proposal that the landward part of Lewis Estate should be handed over to a public trust to be administered for the benefit of the inhabitants'. But in order to bridge its anticipated operating deficit, the district committee felt, any such trust would require assistance – 'for a few years at least' – from government. This assistance, it became clear when district committee representatives met with Ronald Munro Ferguson, Viscount Novar, Secretary of State for Scotland, would not be forthcoming. Shortly afterwards, a majority of committee members voted to reject the Leverhulme proposal. Over the next year or two, as a result, the bulk of the island was divided into several separate estates and auctioned off at knock-down prices – often amounting to no more than two or three pennies an acre. Harris, which Leverhulme had added to his Hebridean landholdings in 1919 and which he retained a little longer, was disposed of in the same way.

If in retrospect this seems an opportunity lost, it should not be allowed to overshadow what was accomplished around Stornoway where, with a seemingly sizeable revenue base to be had for the taking, the burgh's town councillors took the lead in establishing a trust that promptly accepted ownership of the 70,000 acres

I might say at once that it is impossible for me to entertain the proposal that payments for the purpose of meeting … a deficit on the working of the [landward part of the Lewis] Estate should be met by the Board of Agriculture, the Board of Health or any other department [of government]. This decision rests on general grounds of principle, and I do not think it can cause surprise.

Ronald Munro Ferguson, Viscount Novar, Secretary of State for Scotland, September 1923: Roger Hutchinson, The Soapman: Lewis, Harris and Lord Leverhulme, Birlinn, 2003.

Stornoway Harbour.

Lord Leverhulme made available to it. Today the Stornoway Trust – consisting of ten trustees voted into office by an electorate comprising every adult living on the trust's estate – remains in being. The trust's factor or manager, Iain Maciver, along with other members of the organisation's five-strong administrative team, is based in a substantial set of offices, Leverhulme House, overlooking Stornoway Harbour. Ask Iain Maciver, who combines factorial duties with management of his croft at Laxay on the road from Stornoway to Harris, about the Stornoway Trust's present-day significance and his reply is ready: 'Ever since community ownership began to take off in the Highlands and Islands in the 1990s, there have been plenty of people decrying it on the basis that ownership of this sort can't and won't work long-term. The Stornoway Trust proves these people wrong. It's now nearly ninety years since the trust was established – and we're still here.'

Iain Maciver, factor or manager of the Stornoway Trust.

The longevity of the Stornoway Trust is apparent from the row upon row of neatly filed and recently reorganised documents lining its office walls. But for all its apparent solidity, the trust has had its difficulties. The expectations of the long-dead town councillors who took the lead in getting the trust off the ground in 1923 proved over-optimistic and, during much of the Stornoway Trust's first half-century, income failed to match outgoings. Year after year, capital assets such as the trust's farms and much of its housing stock, which cash-strapped trustees could not afford to refurbish, were disposed of in order to balance the books. 'It's hard to see what else could have been done,' Iain Maciver comments. 'Help of the kind that government agencies have given to more recent community ownership ventures just wasn't there. The trust had to rely completely on its own resources. These resources didn't include any really substantial income streams until 1973.'

That year, with the North Sea oil boom getting underway, the Stornoway Trust concluded a deal with the Fred Olsen group, a Norwegian conglomerate. The company wanted to establish a fabrication yard to help meet demand for oil production platforms and associated equipment. The site selected was Arnish, a coastal location just south of Stornoway and well inside the Stornoway Trust's estate. The trust's then factor, Iain Maciver's predecessor, rather than sell the Arnish site, which would have commanded a high price, insisted on leasing it. And for all that the Arnish yard – now in the hands of the latest of several recent operators – has had a chequered history, it continues to provide Lewis people with jobs and the Stornoway Trust with a welcome source of revenue. Business and industrial parks have been developed by the trust in order to create other such sources – and, for the same reason, a lot of time and effort has been invested in plans to establish large-scale wind farms on trust land. Some of these plans, as Iain Maciver acknowledges, have attracted a great deal of local opposition – because of their possibly adverse impact on the Lewis environment – and have failed, as a result, to come to fruition. But the Stornoway Trust's factor, and the trustees to whom he answers, remain convinced that the trust must press on with efforts to secure an income from renewables-related development – an income which, Iain Maciver is convinced, would be big enough to boost the overall performance of Lewis's presently struggling economy. Trustees standing for election on this platform, Iain Maciver points out, have been invariably successful.

The Stornoway Trust is certainly unique in the Highlands and probably in Britain. It is a body looking after an estate … which is wholly in community ownership … Until recently the Trust did little other than act as a caretaking body, despite the fact that it had powers to develop its assets. This was because … income was limited … In recent years the financial situation of the Trust has improved as a result of the rents available from the onshore, oil-related industrial activity at Arnish Point, at the mouth of Stornoway Harbour. This fresh influx of cash has enabled the Trust to launch a programme of activity which is now yielding impressive results.

Frank Thompson, 'Land in Community Ownership: Sixty Years of the Stornoway Trust', in, John Hulbert (ed), Land: Ownership and Use, Andrew Fletcher Society, 1986.

The Stornoway Trust's Woodland Centre.

I do not see why funds from central government should not be made available for the community ownership of land. I am confident that, provided those responsible got the geographical areas right, community ownership … could be the answer to many of the current problems which exist outside the [Stornoway] Trust's area of responsibility, which means in effect the whole of the Highlands and Islands.

D. M. MacIver, Stornoway Trust factor, quoted in, Frank Thompson, 'Land in Community Ownership: Sixty Years of the Stornoway Trust', in, John Hulbert (ed), **Land: Ownership and Use,** *Andrew Fletcher Society, 1986.*

The Stornoway Trust is a member of Community Land Scotland on exactly the same basis as the Isle of Gigha Heritage Trust. But the two are by no means identical – and not just because the Stornoway Trust is answerable to some sixty times more people than its Gigha counterpart. 'Even as late as 1993 when I took up my post here,' Iain Maciver says, 'there were elderly people who, when they came into our office to pay the rents due on their crofts, would recall how they'd heard their parents or grandparents – the generation who remembered the beginnings of the Stornoway Trust – talk about how good it was to be a tenant of the trust in comparison with being a tenant of one of the mostly absentee landlords who bought the rest of Lewis at the close of the Leverhulme era. That doesn't happen now. Even second-hand memories of what happened in the 1920s have faded, and perhaps that's what makes for the biggest difference between our trust and the one in Gigha. There community ownership's still

Stornoway Trust land with, in the background, the Arnish fabrication yard, an important source of trust revenue since the 1970s.

new, still exciting. Here it's taken for granted. That makes our job harder. It's easy to see what community ownership's done for Gigha. Here, because we've been in business for so long, people can't make comparisons with the way things were previously. But I've no doubt that the right decision was made in 1923. Yes, there have been failures. But the Stornoway Trust has stayed the course and, overall, done pretty well. Now the challenge is to do still better in the years ahead.'

———————

In 1973, when *The Cheviot, the Stag and the Black, Black Oil* was taken on tour and when the Stornoway Trust was locked in negotiation with the Olsen group, the trust was already fifty years old. But for all that its trustees were in charge of one of the twenty-five largest landed properties in Scotland, neither the Stornoway Trust nor its smaller counterpart in Glendale were regarded as anything other than curiosities – insignificant

Fishing boat leaving Stornoway Harbour.

A rapid increase in state ownership of land was a striking feature of the twentieth century. Whereas in 1872 just 0.3 per cent of Scotland was in public ownership, by 1979 public bodies and nationalised industries owned and leased 16.8 per cent of the country.

Charles Warren, **Managing Scotland's Natural Environment,** *Edinburgh University Press, 2009.*

The Scottish labour movement requires a land use policy based on the principle of public ownership.

Jim Sillars MP, (Labour: South Ayrshire), 'Land Ownership and Land Nationalisation', in, Gordon Brown (ed), **The Red Paper on Scotland,** *Edinburgh University Student Publication Board, 1975.*

anomalies in a landownership structure so long in place, and so well entrenched, as to be thought unlikely to be altered. At the heart of that structure, as had been the case for centuries, was the privately owned estate. Typically it ran to many thousands of acres. Often its owner was an absentee – someone living at a distance. And while there were localities still in possession of people descended from clan chiefs, this was exceptional. Most Highlands and Islands lairds or their immediate predecessors had bought into the region – with many estates, on the west coast and in the islands in particular, changing hands every few years.

For much of the twentieth century, in the Highlands and Islands as in the rest of the United Kingdom, there was just one alternative to ownership of land by private interests – ownership by government or its agencies. Government's first large-scale acquisitions consisted of the estates and farms purchased, mostly between 1900 and 1925, by the Congested Districts Board and the Board of Agriculture for Scotland. By the 1970s, the land thus taken over was administered by the Department of Agriculture and Fisheries for Scotland (DAFS). The department's landholdings, however, had long since been dwarfed by those in the hands of the Forestry Commission. Set up in 1919 by the Conservative-Liberal coalition which also passed that year's Land Settlement Act, the Forestry Commission, like the Department of Agriculture's predecessor bodies, was empowered to acquire land – in the commission's case in order to afforest it – and did so on a large scale both in the 1920s and, still more, in the two or three decades following the Second World War. Other public sector bodies, notably the Nature Conservancy Council (afterwards Scottish Natural Heritage) and the HIDB, also possessed landholdings in the Highlands and Islands. But the Forestry Commission and DAFS between them accounted for the overwhelming bulk of state-owned land in the region. On the political left in Scotland, the initial source of renewed pressure for reform in the 1970s, there was a general assumption that such reform should consist principally of adding further to the acreage already in government control.

This was an underlying theme of *The Cheviot, the Stag and the Black, Black Oil.* More explicit demands to the same effect were contained in *The Red Paper on Scotland* edited in 1975 by Gordon Brown whose career would culminate in his becoming

Britain's prime minister and who, at this point, was already attracting attention in his role as the first student to have been elected rector of Edinburgh University. His *Red Paper*, Brown wrote, was intended to expose 'extremes of wealth and poverty' including the 'inequality' revealed by 'new and important evidence of the concentration of land ownership in the Highlands and Islands'. This evidence was collected by John McEwen, a retired forester who had been born in Aberfeldy in 1887 and whose subsequent book, *Who Owns Scotland?*, published in 1977, did more than any other publication to boost land reform's prospects. 'Mr McEwen, at 90, is sharply and coherently radical in his view of what should be done,' the journalist Neal Ascherson noted in a review of John McEwen's book in *The Scotsman*. 'He believes in eventual nationalisation of the land.'

John McEwen's findings, and his policy recommendations, attracted more attention in the Highlands and Islands than they might otherwise have done because of the prominence they got in a recently-launched newspaper. This was the *West Highland Free Press*, established in Skye in 1972 and for a lengthy period thereafter edited by one of its youthful founders, Brian Wilson. The *Free Press*'s political stance, in the 1970s and since, is encapsulated in the Gaelic slogan carried on its masthead, *An Tir, an Canan 'sna Daoine* – The Land, the Language and the People. This had been one of the mottoes of the Highland Land League and its adoption by the *West Highland Free Press* signalled the arrival on the Highlands and Islands scene of a weekly which set out – in a manner not experienced in the region since the Land League's demise some eighty years before – to highlight the injustices inherent, as the *Free Press* saw it, in the concentrated pattern of ownership revealed in detail by John McEwen's researches.

As is indicated by this book's many references to him, Brian Wilson's role in relation both to the cause of Highlands and Islands land reform in general, and to the emergence of the community ownership movement in particular, cannot be overestimated. As a campaigning journalist in the 1970s and early 1980s, he exposed and harried those lairds whose management, or mismanagement, of their estates was to result – as later chapters recount – in residents of these estates beginning to embrace, however tentatively at first, the possibility of their becoming their own landlords. Later, as an increasingly influential Labour MP and, between 1997 and 2005, a government

All my life I have been close to the land. There is, however, nothing soft or sentimental in my attitude towards it, rather a deep, growing concern … for the way it has been managed, leading to its present degraded, underdeveloped condition. This is due to the fact of ownership, in the main, by powerful, selfish, antisocial landlords.

John McEwen, Who Owns Scotland?, Edinburgh University Student Publications Board, 1977.

A crofter at work at Bail' an Truseil, Lewis, one of the island localities where community ownership, though turned down in the 1920s, has now been accomplished.

minister, Brian Wilson played a major part in ensuring that the community land trusts then emerging in different parts of the Highlands and Islands got both the political support and the financial backing needed to ensure their success.

In the 1970s, however, all this was far in the future. Brian Wilson, John McEwen and Gordon Brown were members of the Labour Party. But Labour nationally, despite (or perhaps because of) the party being then in power at Westminster, showed little interest in embarking on the further round of land reform that Brown endorsed and McEwen and Wilson urged repeatedly – the Labour administrations of that era, headed by Harold Wilson and James Callaghan, intervening in this area of policy only to enact crofting reforms which, in response to pressure from various crofting bodies, made it possible for individual crofters to take ownership of their crofts.

The way was thus opened for calls for action on land to be made by the Scottish National Party (SNP) which, in the course of the 1970s, had become for the first time a serious contender for power in Scotland. Although even the most rudimentary acquaintance with Highlands and Islands history makes nonsense of the proposition that a Scottish-born laird is automatically to be preferred to one from another country, interest in land reform on the part of the SNP was heightened in the later 1970s by a marked upsurge in overseas participation in the Highlands and Islands land market – with a growing number of estates then passing into the hands of Dutch, German, Swiss, Arab and other non-UK purchasers. This trend towards foreign ownership of Scotland, nationalists asserted, would be halted by the devolved Scottish Assembly which James Callaghan's Labour administration, under electoral pressure from the SNP, had committed itself to creating. But when the proposed assembly failed to gain sufficient backing in a 1979 referendum, when Labour shortly afterwards lost power and when a Conservative government headed by Margaret Thatcher took office, it looked as if land reform would not happen for the foreseeable future.

The Thatcher administration was committed to shrinking the state by denationalising industries taken into public ownership by earlier governments. Hence the privatisation, between 1984 and 1987, of British Telecom, British Gas and

Control of the ownership and use of natural resources is frequently a major political issue … In many cases, the external ownership of land is seen as a very much greater threat than the external exploitation of other natural resources. For reasons of social psychology, the land is an asset which is vested with particular, almost symbolic, significance. The external ownership of land may be perceived as being little short of external control of territory, and there is consequently a particular sensitivity to the issue, irrespective of whether there is any real difference in the use to which land is put under external or domestic ownership.

Tony Carty and John Ferguson, 'Land', in, Tony Carty and Alexander McCall Smith (eds), **Power and Manoeuvrability: The International Implications of an Independent Scotland,** *Q Press, 1978.*

British Airways. Although the Forestry Commission was not privatised outright, the commission was obliged by a Forestry Act of 1981 to begin a land disposal programme intended to result in the sale of hundreds of individual forests – or parts of forests – to private interests. Instead of the area of land in public ownership being increased in the manner envisaged by the left-wing land reformers of the 1970s, then, this area began to shrink – not least in the Highlands and Islands where, by the mid-1980s, it seemed likely that the crofting estates run by the Department of Agriculture and Fisheries for Scotland might be next in line for privatisation or disposal. If that were to happen, this book's author suggested in 1986, perhaps the DAFS estates, rather than being sold to the highest bidder, should be handed over to the people living on them. This suggestion was made in the belief that no Conservative politician would have the slightest interest in adopting such a course. But that was a misjudgement. By the start of the 1990s, community ownership – along the lines of the Stornoway Trust – was

The Isle of Raasay is one of the many Highlands and Islands localities brought into state ownership in the early twentieth century.

being investigated and advocated by Conservative ministers. The ministers in question began by promoting such ownership only in circumstances where the previous owner was the state. Eventually, however, they were to welcome – and permit public agencies to assist – the acquisition of privately-owned estates by the communities resident on them. In the later 1990s and into the twenty-first century, other political parties would keep community ownership on the political agenda. But it was the Conservative government of the 1980s which made the first serious attempt in modern times to get communities in the Highlands and Islands to take control of substantial areas of land.

'At the end of the day,' said Mr George Younger, the then Secretary of State for Scotland [in 1983], 'the overriding objective must be to harness the creative energy and skills of people in local communities so that they will be able to maintain and enhance the life of these communities.' These are admirable sentiments. And any sale of the DAFS estates will offer the ideal opportunity to put them into practice. Consider, for instance, the island of Vatersay, bought by the Congested Districts Board in 1909 … What better way could there be of 'harnessing the creative energy and skills' of such a locality than making its people entirely responsible for its management? … Just how community ownership might be effected is a matter for detailed discussion – although the Stornoway Trust, which manages an entire Hebridean parish on behalf of its inhabitants, provides on eminently satisfactory model. A Conservative government which is committed to promoting self-help and encouraging self-reliance would surely do well to approach any privatisation of the [DAFS] estates on the basis that they be privatised in the direction of their occupants.

James Hunter, 'The DAFS Crofting Estates: A Case for Community Control', in, John Hulbert (ed), **Land: Ownership and Use,** *Andrew Fletcher Society, 1986.*

Bill Ritchie of the Assynt Crofters Trust.

3

WE HAVE WON THE LAND

Community ownership initiative on government-owned
estates in Skye and Raasay
Assynt Crofters Trust
Culag Community Woodland Trust
Kylesku Crofters Trust
Assynt Foundation
Borve and Annishader Township
Crofting Trust Advisory Service
Melness Crofters Estate
Laggan Forestry Trust
North West Mull Community Woodland Company
Bute Community Land Company
Transfer of Crofting Estates Act
West Harris Trust

Croft land in West Harris – the first state-owned crofting property to be brought into community ownership.

CHAPTER THREE
We have won the land

Community ownership initiative on government-owned estates in Skye and Raasay § Assynt Crofters Trust § Culag Community Woodland Trust Kylesku Crofters Trust § Assynt Foundation § Borve and Annishader Township Crofting Trust Advisory Service § Melness Crofters Estate Laggan Forestry Trust § North West Mull Community Woodland Company Bute Community Land Company § Transfer of Crofting Estates Act West Harris Trust

The Scottish Crofters Union (SCU), formed in the mid-1980s 'to promote and protect the interests of crofting communities throughout the Highlands and Islands', aimed from the outset – if only because, given the electoral dominance of successive Tory administrations, this was the only available option – to work constructively with Conservative politicians.* In Russell Sanderson, the Borders peer and businessman who, as Minister of State at the Scottish Office from 1987 to 1990, was responsible for matters affecting both crofting and the Highlands and Islands more widely, the SCU found someone receptive to arguments advanced on behalf of the union's several thousand members. Those arguments were intended to make sense in Conservative terms. When the grants and loans which crofters got to help them build new homes on their crofts were under threat, for example, the SCU made the point – successfully – that such assistance was, in fact, a highly cost-effective way of contributing to the much canvassed Conservative objective of enabling as many people as possible to become home-owners. The union approached the possible disposal of the government's crofting estates in the same spirit.

Addressing the SCU's annual conference in Benbecula in March 1989, Lord Sanderson underlined the government's wish to rid itself of its crofting estates by

---

* A declaration of interest. I was part-time secretary of the Crofters Union Steering Group which set up the SCU during 1984 and 1985. From 1986 to 1990, I was the union's director.

persuading crofters on these estates to buy their crofts. Individual crofters had been granted a right to purchase their holdings from landowners (whether public or private) by the Crofting Reform Act of 1976, a Labour measure; but few DAFS tenants had chosen to do this. Their reasoning was similar to that of their predecessors who, at the start of the twentieth century, had rejected the 50-year purchase deals offered by the Congested Districts Board. To swap a secure tenancy for ownership was to gain very little and, potentially, to lose a lot – in that much of the financial assistance available to crofters was less easily obtained by owner-occupiers than by tenants. He was aware of this 'fear of the loss of access to grants', Russell Sanderson told his 180-strong audience in Benbecula, but he wished, the minister stressed, 'to hear of suggestions which might assist those interested in home and land ownership which the government is anxious to promote'. There and then it was put to Lord Sanderson by the SCU that, if the government wanted out from under its ownership of the DAFS crofting estates, then – instead of pushing owner-occupation – ministers should explore ways in which these estates might go into ownership of the sort exemplified by the Stornoway Trust.

When Lord Sanderson indicated to the SCU earlier this year that he was minded to dispose of the Department of Agriculture's crofting estates, we told him bluntly that the introduction of wholesale owner-occupation would not be acceptable to us. Instead we suggested a community-ownership approach along the lines pioneered on the Stornoway Trust estate in Lewis.

Angus MacRae, President, Scottish Crofters Union, November 1989: The Crofter, February 1990.

The future of the Secretary of State's crofting estates has recently attracted considerable interest. The government take the view that they should not continue to hold land which is not required for the purpose for which it was acquired in general more than fifty years ago. This is an anachronism … I am … fully seized of the difficulties of, and possible objections to, owner-occupation … I was accordingly most interested when the possibility of some form of community ownership was raised with me in Benbecula … We consider that there is scope for more direct involvement of crofters in the running of the estates at present owned by the Secretary of State and that local skills, knowledge and interest might be harnessed to achieve this.

Lord Sanderson, Minister of State at the Scottish Office, November 1989: The Crofter, February 1990.

This consultation paper seeks views on the possible transfer of responsibility for some of the Secretary of State's crofting estates to trusts including representatives of crofting interests or to some other form of community ownership … Transfer to a trust would provide local communities with greater control over, and greater responsibility for, their own affairs, with the scope to be more responsive to local sensitivities, and with greater ability to take account of local interests and opportunities.

Department of Agriculture and Fisheries for Scotland, **Consultation Paper on Possible Disposal of the Secretary of State for Scotland's Crofting Estates to Community Ownership,** *February 1990.*

Speaking in Inverness in November 1989, Russell Sanderson made clear that he had been persuaded by the SCU's contention that, in a crofting context anyway, community ownership was likely to be preferred to what the union's president, Angus MacRae, a crofter from North Strome in Wester Ross, called 'wholesale owner-occupation'. The Department of Agriculture, Lord Sanderson revealed, would shortly begin consulting on how the government's crofting estates might be got into community ownership. This consultation duly got underway at the start of 1990.

The news that crofters were to be given the chance to take charge of the Department of Agriculture's crofting estates was greeted positively across the political spectrum in the Highlands and Islands. Charles Kennedy, Liberal Democrat MP for Ross, Cromarty and Skye, called the proposal 'a breath of fresh air' that could result in DAFS 'handing the land back to the people'. Calum Macdonald, Labour MP for the Western Isles, believed the SCU deserved congratulation for having taken 'the debate about land use and ownership in the Highlands to a stage where even this government [whose disposals of Forestry Commission land to the private sector Macdonald deplored] are conceding the principle of community ownership'. Brian Wilson, who had become Labour MP for the Ayrshire constituency of Cunninghame North in 1987 but who was still a regular contributor to the *West Highland Free Press*, commented of the Sanderson initiative: 'It is precisely because it merits a positive response that it must be explored in great detail.' Just such exploration, however, was to reveal difficulties of a sort calculated to give many crofters pause for thought.

A consultation paper issued by the Scottish Office in February 1990 indicated that, if community ownership of the government's crofting estates was to proceed, this should be on the basis of a pilot project involving the DAFS estates on the islands of Skye and Raasay. There were seven such estates, purchased at various points between 1904 and 1939, extending to just under 150,000 acres and tenanted by some 630 crofters. In order to provide those crofters with the fullest possible information about what community ownership might entail, the SCU, with financial support from the HIDB, commissioned the Arkleton Trust, a rural development charity, to report on 'the legal and practical implications' of what was on offer. A four-strong team, headed by the Arkleton Trust's programme director, John Bryden, an agricultural economist, and including a further economist as well as two lawyers, spent several weeks investigating administrative arrangements on the government's Skye and Raasay crofting estates – while also meeting and talking with affected crofters. Their report, issued in June 1990, highlighted a number of substantial impediments in the way of community ownership.

It was assumed by all concerned that, if the DAFS estates were to be sold by government to crofting trusts, then the price paid by those trusts should be determined in accordance with the formula laid down by the Crofting Reform Act of 1976 for working out the capital value of a single croft – this formula giving a figure equivalent to fifteen times the croft's annual rent. If calculated in the same way, the selling price of the DAFS estates on Skye and Raasay would be in the region of £500,000.

How might crofters raise this amount? And beyond that, how were crofters to meet the annual running costs of estates from which, as the Arkleton team found, DAFS were deriving a total yearly income, from crofting rents and other sources, of around £41,000 – while simultaneously spending £155,000 annually on management?

While the acquisition cost problem could be solved by government simply giving its crofting estates to community bodies free of charge, something the DAFS consultation paper of February 1990 suggested might be done, the resulting organisations were then unlikely to be able to meet administrative costs – the February consultation paper having warned that, in the event of a cost-free transfer of ownership, 'there would not be a strong case for further government support' being made available to newly-created trusts.

Prior to the Arkleton team starting work, Angus MacRae of the SCU had spoken about what happened in Lewis in 1923 when islanders, other than those in the vicinity of Stornoway, had felt obliged to turn down the opportunity of community ownership. While there had been good reasons for their so doing, the union president told the SCU's annual conference in March 1990, it was impossible, with hindsight, to regard Lewis people's 1923 decision as anything other than 'a tragic error'. Angus MacRae continued: 'Whatever else we do, we must not make another such mistake.'

Ironically, however, Skye and Raasay crofters confronted in 1990 exactly the same difficulty as that faced by their Lewis counterparts of nearly seventy years before. They could not see how any prospective crofting trust could pay its way. And while the Arkleton team were of the view that, under community ownership, the administrative costs of the government's crofting estates on Skye and Raasay could be cut by as much as three-quarters, this was hypothetical.

Opinion among Raasay and Skye crofters as to what should happen next was divided. In some localities there was more support for community ownership than in others and, overall, younger crofters were more inclined than the elderly to favour change. As debate continued, however, scepticism about, or hostility to, the community ownership option became more prevalent. The SCU duly reported to government that, while DAFS tenants on Skye and Raasay would certainly opt for community

Staffin in Skye is one of the localities where crofters living on state-owned land turned down the chance of community ownership in 1990.

ownership if the alternative was an open market disposal of DAFS properties, their preference was to leave things as they were. This wish was granted. Although the SCU was informed formally by the Scottish Office towards the end of 1990 that 'the sale of the Secretary of State's [crofting] estates on the open market [had] not been ruled out', no such sale took place. A year later, the Scottish Office announced that, in view of the crofting response to the government's community ownership initiative, this initiative would – for the moment at least – be put on hold.

At the time, Iain Maciver, now the Stornoway Trust's factor but then president of the SCU in succession to Angus MacRae, told the *West Highland Free Press*: 'A good opportunity has been lost.' That is still Iain Maciver's view. It is one that is shared by Simon Fraser, a partner in a Stornoway legal firm, Anderson, MacArthur & Co. A crofter as well as a lawyer with extensive experience of estate administration,

West Harris was the first government-owned crofting locality to opt for community ownership – but a long time after the failed initiative in Skye and Raasay.

Simon Fraser was a key member of the Arkleton Trust enquiry team the SCU hired at the start of the attempt to establish community ownership on a large scale in Raasay and Skye. 'What struck most people at the time about our findings was the enormous sum the Department of Agriculture and Fisheries were spending every year on estate management,' Simon Fraser comments. 'The department, of course, operated bureaucratically with decision after decision being referred further and further up the organisation – often all the way to Edinburgh. Their Skye and Raasay estates could easily have been run by crofters for a fraction of what these estates were costing the government. But people, understandably enough, were reluctant to accept this. There was a widespread perception that Highlands and Islands estates were immensely costly to manage and that, as a result, they could be owned and operated only by well-financed public bodies or by very wealthy individuals. Today we know better. Today we're well aware that all sorts of communities can run estates both efficiently and profitably – delivering a whole set of benefits in the process. But in the early 1990s, this was something that had still to be proved.'

While in Skye to explore ways in which the DAFS estates there might be brought into community ownership, Simon Fraser co-operated closely with Andrew Robertson, a Glasgow-based solicitor who had been added to the Arkleton Trust inquiry team because his work with grassroots housing associations in Glasgow had made him an expert in charity law and in how to equip community-based organisations with the most appropriate institutional structures. Jointly, the two lawyers examined various means of ensuring the viability, durability and openness of the trust or trusts which, at that stage, they expected to take over the 150,000 acres on offer to Raasay and Skye crofters. Any such trust, Robertson and Fraser concluded, should take the form of a company limited by guarantee. On their being formed, they added, such companies should at once seek charitable status.

A company limited by guarantee has no shareholders. In a community ownership context, this closes off the possibility of shares being sold or transferred to people or institutions outside the locality the company is set up to serve. A company limited by guarantee, however, does have members. Their financial liabilities are restricted to the nominal sum, usually a pound, they guarantee to make available in the event of the company being wound up. But their being members gives them control of the company by entitling them to define its objectives, elect its directors and restrict its membership to people living in a particular place.

If, then, crofters on one or other of the DAFS estates on Skye and Raasay had opted for community ownership in 1990, Andrew Robertson and Simon Fraser would have recommended that the title to any land they took on should be vested in a company limited by guarantee. As it was, this did not happen, and the documentation dealing with how community ownership might be brought into being by these means was filed away in Simon Fraser's Stornoway office. In December 1991, when the Scottish Office announced formally that its proposed transfer of government-owned land to crofters had been abandoned, it seemed probable that the file in question would remain closed for a long time. Just six months later, however, Simon Fraser got a telephone call that led to its being at once reopened. This telephone call came from Bill Ritchie, a crofter at Achmelvich on the west coast of Sutherland and treasurer of the SCU's Assynt branch. Most of the branch's several dozen members were tenants of the North Lochinver Estate which had just been advertised for sale. At meetings called to discuss the implications of this sale, Bill Ritchie said, crofters living on the North Lochinver Estate had decided to launch their own bid for the property. Their aim was to bring the estate into community ownership, and they wanted Simon Fraser to act on their behalf.

———————

When its crofting tenants decided to try to buy the North Lochinver Estate, they were doing something little short of revolutionary. Community ownership had been achieved in Glendale as a result of crofters acquiring land made available to them by government. Community ownership had taken shape in the Stornoway area when people there accepted Lord Leverhulme's gift of the land in their vicinity. But not until crofters got together on a summer evening in Assynt in 1992 had any group of Highlands and Islands residents initiated their own open-market bid for a privately-owned estate of the sort that had always previously been bought and sold without reference to, or interference from, the people living on it.

Who owns this landscape? –
The millionaire who bought it or
the poacher staggering downhill in
the early morning
with a deer on his back?

Norman MacCaig, 'A Man in Assynt', 1969.

One need only enter Assynt and see the great sphinx-like mass of Suilven to sense the atmosphere of unreality, almost fantasy, which pervades the character of the people who live there. Mountains such as Quinag, Canisp, Ben More Assynt, Cul Mor, Cul Beag, Stac Polly and Conival have immense power to impress and serve to emphasise that man himself is perhaps the alien in this landscape.

John Clegg & Co., **Sale Particulars: North Lochinver Estate,** *June 1992.*

'*Who owns this landscape?*'

The parish of Assynt had suffered greatly during the Highland Clearances. The royal commission of inquiry which looked into crofting grievances in 1883 was told that, on the orders of the couple who later became the first Duke and Duchess of Sutherland, 'over fifty' of the locality's settlements ceased to exist in the course of the nineteenth century's opening decades. Recent research by historian Malcolm Bangor-Jones has identified more than thirty of these – inland spots, some of them occupied for many hundreds of years, from which families who did not quit Sutherland after their eviction were moved to overcrowded crofting townships on Assynt's Atlantic coast.

Assynt remained part of the Sutherland Estate until 1913 when the fourth Duke of Sutherland sold the district to Major-General William Stewart, a Canadian of Sutherland descent. This was the first of a series of ownership changes lasting into the mid-1930s when the estate was acquired by the Vestey family, owners of a meat-based business empire operating across the UK, South America, North America, Australia, New Zealand and South Africa.

In 1989 Assynt's then owner, Edmund Vestey, divided his estate in two. Inland areas were retained. The coastal strip – the part of Assynt occupied, as it had been since the clearances, by crofters – was put up for sale. Named North Lochinver Estate, this new creation, extending to just over 21,000 acres and described as a 'wilderness' of 'astonishing beauty' in the sale particulars, was bought in three separate lots for more than £1 million by a Swedish company, Scandinavian Property Services (SPS) Ltd. Three years later, SPS Ltd was bankrupt and its assets were in the hands of a liquidator who promptly put the company's Assynt landholdings back on the market – this time in seven lots.

The North Lochinver Estate was almost entirely under crofting tenure and consisted, in effect, of thirteen townships – Torbreck, Achmelvich, Clachtoll, Clashmore, Balchladich, Raffin, Achnacarnin, Culkein, Stoer, Clashnessie, Drumbeg, Culkein Drumbeg and Nedd. Those townships were occupied by a total of around 140 crofters. They were unsettled by the second sale in three years of the land around them.

Over fifty townships in this parish [of Assynt] were made desolate, and the tenants sent hither and thither over the face of the earth, and when they found a resting place at all in their native land, it was on the poorest scraps, rocks and bogs, and often put in amongst ... [other] crofters, subdividing their lots [meaning crofts], and intensifying their poverty.

William Mackenzie, labourer, Clashnessie, giving evidence to the Commissioners of Inquiry into the Condition of the Crofters and Cottars in the Highlands and Islands of Scotland, July 1883.

The clearances are central to an understanding of Highland history ... They were often achieved by the use of force, brought a radical alteration to Highland society and caused great upheaval ... They continue to be controversial and indeed are as much a present-day issue as a past episode. The Sutherland Clearances are among the most notorious. Assynt, a parish in north-west Sutherland which has become celebrated in recent years as a landmark in the movement to community ownership of land, was part of the Sutherland Estate. Between

1812 and 1821, Assynt was cleared for the Marquis and Marchioness of Stafford [afterwards created Duke and Duchess of Sutherland].

Malcolm Bangor-Jones, The Assynt Clearances, *Assynt Press, 2001.*

What does a meat-packer in the Argentine, a merchant seaman on the high seas, a docker in London, a container-lorry driver on the motorways have in common with a crofter in Lochinver?

Nothing at all.

Wrong. They are all wholly-owned subsidiaries of the Vestey Brothers.

John McGrath, The Cheviot, the Stag and the Black, Black Oil, *Eyre Methuen, 1981.*

They were still more unsettled by the potential fragmentation of the North Lochinver Estate and the consequent possibility of some townships ending up with not just one, but two or more, absentee landlords.

When, on 6 June 1992, members of the SCU's Assynt branch met to consider how best to respond to this threat, they did so in the context created by the sometimes ferocious arguments that had gone on both inside and outside the union about whether or not the DAFS estates in Skye and Raasay should go into community ownership. That debate had centred on the fate of land in public, not private, hands. But the Department of Agriculture's consultation paper of February 1990 – circulated in the wake of the government's decision to offer its crofting estates on Raasay and Skye to their tenants – had asked for reactions to the possibility of the community ownership principle being applied to croft land other than that belonging to the Secretary of State for Scotland. There had been considerable comment along the lines that this would be a very good idea – a much better idea, some people said, than denationalising, as they saw it, state-owned properties. When, during 1991, the Dalmore Estate in Lewis and the Strollamus Estate in Skye were advertised for sale, there had duly been some talk to the effect that their residents should have a stab at bringing them into community ownership. Nothing came of this. But the idea that such an attempt could be made was in circulation. What was needed were people sufficiently motivated and sufficiently organised to make a reality of what had previously been little more than theoretical discussion. A set of just such people emerged in Assynt during June 1992.

Their leaders were the three principal office-bearers of the SCU's Assynt branch: Bill Ritchie who, as already mentioned, was the branch's treasurer; Allan MacRae, its chairman; and John MacKenzie, its vice-chairman. At the branch's meeting on 6 June it had been decided that MacRae, MacKenzie and Ritchie, in collaboration with colleagues drawn from each of the thirteen townships on the North Lochinver Estate, should immediately constitute a steering group mandated, as a union branch press release of 9 June put it, 'to fight [the] break-up' of the property. 'Crofters in Assynt,' this press release went on, '[have] expressed their …

determination to resist the attempted sale in small lots of … [the North Lochinver] Estate. The crofters [have] agreed to pursue the possibility of establishing a trust to purchase the land.' Soon the projected trust, in the shape of exactly the sort of company limited by guarantee that would have been constituted in Skye and Raasay had community ownership gone ahead there, was in place. The new organisation, named the Assynt Crofters Trust, engaged Simon Fraser as its legal adviser and, towards the end of July, invited the wider public, in Scotland and beyond, to help with its fund-raising efforts.

The response to this invitation exceeded all expectation. This was in large part because press coverage of developments in Assynt was extensive, continuing and – for the most part – sympathetic. While it may or may not be true that well-wishers took to collecting cash in buckets in Glasgow pubs, interest in what was being

Assynt croft land.

The North Lochinver Estate was sold by the millionaire Vestey family to a foreign property company … That company is now bankrupt and our croft land is being broken up and offered for sale again in small lots. The land is virtually all croft land. We … have resolved to band together to buy the estate, not for reason [of] … political or romantic sentiment but because we believe that, to give our crofting communities the best chance of surviving and prospering in the future, control of our resources – especially the land – will be our best chance. [We] are forming a company limited by guarantee – to be known as The Assynt Crofters Trust – and we hope to achieve charitable status. Membership and control of the Trust will be restricted to the crofting tenants of the North Lochinver Estate.

Assynt Crofters Trust Fund Appeal, *July 1992.*

Fundamental to what we are setting out to do is that it's the people on the ground who will make the decisions on what happens here.

Allan MacRae, September 1992: **West Highland Free Press,** *11 September 1992.*

attempted in Assynt was certainly widespread. A week after its launch, the trust's appeal had netted £15,000. Four months later, some £56,000 had been received and another £74,000 – every penny of which was to be forthcoming – had been pledged. Recalling the stream of envelopes containing cheques, postal orders and banknotes that began to be delivered to his Achmelvich croft, Bill Ritchie comments: 'What was really moving was the support we got from so many very ordinary, and by no means well-off, people. I remember in particular a letter from an old age pensioner. The letter wished us well. Attached to it were three postage stamps. These, the writer said, might be of some help to us.'

Bill Ritchie of the Assynt Crofters Trust on his croft at Achmelvich.

John MacKenzie of the Assynt Crofters Trust.

I want to pay tribute … to David Ross of *The Herald* newspaper and Iain MacDonald of BBC [Scotland] … [M]uch of the success of our campaign to raise public financial support and political enthusiasm was due to their help.

John MacKenzie, addressing the Gaelic Society of Inverness, March 2011.

Clearly, if the local crofters were to come up with economically viable plans, and show a strong unity of purpose by forming a trust to take control of the situation, then I am sure the council would want to look very seriously at ways in which we might be able to give assistance.

Peter Peacock, Vice-Convener, Highland Regional Council, June 1992: The Herald, *11 June 1992.*

We are actively supporting this particular bid because it embraces the overall aim of the HIE network to allow the people of the area to realise their full potential through stimulating business development, strengthening the community and raising the quality of life.

Iain Robertson, Chief Executive, Highlands and Islands Enterprise, September 1992: John MacAskill, We Have Won the Land: The Story of the Purchase by the Assynt Crofters Trust of the North Lochinver Estate, *Acair, 1999.*

Public bodies too began to rally round. A key ally from the outset was Highland Regional Council's vice-convener, Peter Peacock, who also chaired the council's finance and budget committees. Subsequently a Labour Member of the Scottish Parliament (MSP) and a minister in the Labour-Liberal Democrat coalitions that had substantial majorities in the first two such parliaments to be elected after Scottish devolution took effect in 1999, Peter Peacock, who stood down as an MSP in early 2011, was afterwards appointed Community Land Scotland's part-time policy director. Reflecting today on Highland Regional Council's support for the Assynt Crofters Trust, Peter comments: 'It seemed to me and to a number of key council colleagues that, if we didn't give public backing to the Assynt crofters, then how could we argue, as we were set on arguing, that other organisations, including Highlands and Islands Enterprise, should do so? HIE, we believed, had to be put under a bit of pressure – otherwise there was every likelihood of its leadership backing away from something so risky and so potentially contentious as community ownership still was at that stage.'

Hence Highland Regional Council's endorsement of, and financial support for, the Assynt Crofters Trust – a development which Simon Fraser was afterwards to say convinced him that the trust could win its battle for the North Lochinver Estate. But if the council's stance was a key factor in the unfolding drama in Assynt, it was also a consequence, Peter Peacock contends, of the political balance in the Highlands and Islands having shifted in ways that made initiatives of the sort the regional council took in 1992 altogether more feasible than they would once have been. Prior to local government reorganisation in 1975, Peter points out, the county councils which then gave way to Highland Regional Council had been run largely by landlords and their allies. 'The new regional council wasn't at all like that,' he says. 'Soon it was controlled by people of a very different sort; older men whose political views had been shaped by wartime military service; younger people who were equally unprepared to kow-tow to lairds; folk who were up for helping Allan MacRae, John MacKenzie, Bill Ritchie and the Assynt Crofters Trust get hold of the North Lochinver Estate.'

Allying the regional council in this way with the Assynt Crofters Trust was intended to help persuade Highlands and Islands Enterprise that the trust was as

Assynt crofts with Suilven in the background.

The economic principle for purchasing the land is to ensure that the income and wealth, which it is capable of generating, stays within the local community. Much of the potential benefits will only be realised in the long term, however, and the crofters are as much interested in providing the next generation with a sounder base as in improving their current economic welfare.

Assynt Crofters Trust, **Business Plan,** *August 1992.*

The estate ... has not previously been run with any employment creation objectives, its sporting value has declined, and there has been no systematic effort to protect or enhance its amenity value to the general public. One part-time job is currently provided by the estate, and the individual concerned lives outwith the area.

Assynt Crofters Trust, **Business Plan,** *August 1992.*

deserving of financial assistance as the more conventional businesses which benefited regularly from HIE aid. Getting HIE on side took a little time – the agency being wary, as Peter Peacock suspected, of involvement in Assynt. When it came, however, HIE's grant of £50,000 to the Assynt Crofters Trust, though not enormous in cash terms, was significant politically. Since HIE was a government agency, its lining up behind the trust demonstrated that neither Conservative ministers nor their civil servants were doing anything to prevent an organisation which answered to them from backing an initiative portrayed widely in the media as the beginnings of a grassroots assault on the longstanding domination of much of the rural Highlands and Islands by absentee landlords – whether individual lairds, as had been the case traditionally, or companies of the SPS type, as was beginning to be more common.

By way of proving – not least to the public sector organisations with whom Ritchie, MacRae and MacKenzie were in increasingly close discussion – that the North Lochinver Estate could be operated successfully by the Assynt Crofters Trust, the trust commissioned a feasibility study and business plan. Because the North Lochinver Estate – certainly in comparison with crofting properties controlled by DAFS – had long been run on a shoestring, the resulting document, produced jointly by an economist and a chartered accountant, threw up none of the obstacles that had confronted proponents of community ownership in Skye and Raasay a year or two earlier. While there was no very obvious way in which the Assynt Crofters Trust could make a lot of money from the assets its members were looking to acquire, neither was there any reason to doubt that, under community ownership, these assets would yield an annual income at least equivalent to the trust's likely outgoings. Thus reassured, the Assynt Crofters Trust set about preparing the bid lodged in early September with John Clegg & Co, the Edinburgh-based land agents handling the sale of the North Lochinver Estate on behalf of the London liquidator whose job it was to deal with the financial mess left behind by the now defunct SPS Ltd.

Thanks to the croft purchase provisions of the 1976 Crofting Reform Act as modified by subsequent court judgements, the North Lochinver Estate's crofting tenants could in principle have bought the property for less than a tenth of its advertised price of

£473,000. The procedures involved, however, would have been complex, time-consuming and not altogether certain. While the possibility of embarking on those procedures was kept open, not least with a view to scaring off rival bidders, the Assynt Crofters Trust was minded, from the start, to offer what its members believed to be a fair market price for the estate. On the basis of information gathered by the consultants responsible for the production of the trust's business plan, such a price was reckoned to be £235,000 – about half of what the liquidator was aiming to get and less than a quarter of what the property had cost Scandinavian Property Services Ltd just three years before.

'Although it didn't seem so to many people at the time,' Simon Fraser recalls, 'the Assynt Crofters Trust was actually in a strong bargaining position. Other prospective purchasers were undoubtedly deterred by the trust's threat that a rival bidder, if successful, would immediately become embroiled in endless legal battles with crofters who'd made it clear that, if outbid, they'd try to buy those parts of the North Lochinver Estate that were under crofting tenure – which was virtually all of it – by taking advantage of the purchase route opened up by the Crofting Reform Act. Of course, the Act hadn't been intended to make a whole estate vulnerable to acquisition in this way. But the Scottish Land Court had interpreted the 1976 legislation in such a manner as to make the possibility a real one.

'The Assynt Crofters Trust,' Simon Fraser continues, 'were also helped greatly by the fact that the North Lochinver Estate was being sold by a liquidator. If the seller had been a still-solvent landlord, then he or she could simply have taken the estate off the market if the trust's offer hadn't come up to expectation. But liquidators don't have that freedom. When disposing of assets, they have to take what they can get – and they have to move reasonably fast. In the event, the Assynt Crofters Trust had to raise its offer more than once. But by early December 1992, the trust had succeeded in buying the North Lochinver Estate for £300,000. That was £65,000 up on the trust's first offer. But it was £173,000 less than the asking price.'

'It seems we have won the land,' Allan MacRae told the celebratory gathering convened in Assynt on the evening of the day, 8 December 1992, that people there

Well, ladies and gentlemen, it seems we have won the land. It certainly is a moment to savour. There is no doubt about that, and … my immediate thoughts are to wish that some of our forebears could be here to share this moment with us. In winning the land, Assynt crofters have struck a historic blow for people on the land throughout the Highlands.

Allan MacRae, Assynt Crofters Trust, at a public meeting in Stoer School, 8 December 1992.

My own overriding emotion at the time, I have to confess, was that of the sense of righting some of the injustices suffered by our forebears, and sadness that my parents and grandparents, as well as my late brother, had not lived to see the day … we took possession of title to the land … What a sense of liberation and achievement to be able to look around over the land upon which our forebears had been mere tenants, living their lives at the whim of culturally insensitive landlords, and over which we now had ownership and almost total control! What an outstanding privilege to have played a small part in these events that have so changed the course of history in our Highlands and Islands!

John MacKenzie, addressing the Gaelic Society of Inverness, March 2011.

They know how to celebrate in Assynt and they were more than entitled to be doing it last night. On a simple, human level the Assynt Crofters Trust's protracted and finally triumphant campaign to buy the North Lochinver Estate is a great story brought to an uplifting climax … At a deeper level, they have beaten a track along which others must surely be tempted to venture. At its end lies an attractive, if not necessarily universal, answer to the perpetual question of land ownership in the Highlands. It is high testimony to [the Assynt Crofters Trust's] skill and determination that, despite setbacks, they ultimately prevailed. In the process, they have built and consolidated a powerful consensus for the concept of community ownership in the Highlands.

Scotsman editorial, 9 December 1992.

heard of the acceptance of their latest offer for the North Lochinver Estate. 'My immediate thoughts,' Allan went on, 'are to wish that some our forebears could be here to share this moment with us'. John MacKenzie too believed strongly that injustices dating back to the clearances had at last been remedied. 'But we did not do what we did in order to get some sort of revenge for what happened in the past,' he insists. 'We were looking to the future and to the opportunity we'd been given to have a real hand in shaping that future.'

When meeting today with John MacKenzie on his croft at Culkein Drumbeg, or with another Assynt Crofters Trust activist, Anne MacCrimmon, on her croft at nearby Drumbeg, it is immediately evident that progress in Assynt, in the years since 1992, has not been as rapid as John and Anne think it should have been. But much has been accomplished nevertheless. Younger people have been got on to a number of crofts. Affordable housing has been provided. The trust has built an office to accommodate its paid staff of two part-timers. More than a million trees have been planted and native woodland has been encouraged to regenerate and expand. Deer stalking and trout fishing have been developed in ways that have created – as is also true of the Assynt Crofters Trust's various afforestation initiatives – local employment. Perhaps most significantly, Assynt Crofters Trust, in partnership with a commercial concern, has constructed – and manages – a hydro electricity plant which is presently delivering around £60,000 annually to its owners.

Standing in the building which houses Assynt Hydro's water-driven generator, John MacKenzie, who worked very hard over several years to make this shared venture a reality, explains the thinking behind the company. 'What we're doing here is generating cash as well as electricity,' John says. 'So far, most of the money made by Assynt Hydro, has gone into paying off the capital cost of pipelines, plant, grid connection and the rest. But soon that will have been done. And soon we'll be renegotiating our current contract with the power utility we're supplying. The price we get will go up, we'll have paid off our debts and we'll be in a position to invest in further development.'

Elsewhere in Assynt, meanwhile, groups other than the Assynt Crofters Trust are making similar plans – the process that began with the purchase of the North Lochinver Estate having since resulted in the community ownership of other large segments of this enormous parish. On his croft at Achmelvich, the southernmost of the various townships bought by crofters in 1992, Bill Ritchie comments: 'One of the great gains brought by community ownership is the way it opens people's minds to all sorts of new possibilities.' Hence, perhaps, the proliferation of community ownership projects in this part of Sutherland.

Culag Community Woodland Trust, formed in 1995, to manage a 100 acre piece of woodland on the outskirts of Lochinver, Assynt's nearest approximation to a town, afterwards bought the 3,000 acre Little Assynt Estate and now employs several people as well as providing training in forestry and land management. At Kylesku, in Assynt's north-eastern corner, the 800 acre township of the same name was taken over by its crofters in 2001. And in 2005 the 44,000 acre Glencanisp and Drumrunie Estates were bought by a further local grouping, the Assynt Foundation, which is progressing a range of initiatives – including the creation of new crofts and, in emulation of the Assynt Crofters Trust, the provision of affordable housing.

Above, left: Assynt Crofters Trust member, Anne MacCrimmon. Right: John MacKenzie in the generating hall of the Assynt Crofters Trust's hydro-electric power station.

Sustaining and expanding native woodland is an Assynt Crofters Trust priority.

Culag Community Woodland Trust (CCWT) was formed in 1995 to manage Culag Wood under a fifty-year lease from the owners, Assynt Estates and Highland Council. CCWT owns the Little Assynt Estate, which it bought in November 2000. In July 2003 CCWT purchased an office to facilitate the smooth running of administration and communication with local residents, visitors and other organisations. It is run by twelve directors drawn from the local community and has an active membership as well as enthusiastic volunteers and staff.

Culag Community Woodland Trust website, June 2011.

The Assynt Foundation was established in advance of the landmark community buy-out of the Glencanisp and Drumrunie Estates in the parish of Assynt … In June 2005 the community of Assynt bought these estates, 44,000 acres of stunningly beautiful natural land from the Vestey family … The area includes the magnificent mountains, Suilven, Canisp, Cul Mor and Cul Beag, the beautiful Victorian hunting lodge, Glencanisp Lodge, and an awe-inspiring, wildlife-rich world of lochans, rivers and hills. Our objectives … are to manage community land and associated assets for the benefit of the community and the public in general.

Assynt Foundation website, June 2011.

On the basis that Highland estates could only be run successfully by individuals or organisations with deep pockets, there were those who thought in 1992 that the Assynt Crofters Trust was bound to fail. 'I should think the crofters in Assynt will live to regret buying the [North Lochinver] Estate,' one experienced land agent, Neil Graham-Campbell of Finlayson-Hughes, told a national newspaper. Others were more optimistic – Brian Wilson, for example, expressing 'the intense hope', which was shared widely, that the Assynt Crofters Trust's achievement would 'set a whole movement rolling'. The first signs that such a movement was indeed developing became apparent in Skye at the start of 1993.

One of the SCU's achievements had been to secure in 1991 a Crofter Forestry Act which enabled crofting communities to establish plantations on hill grazings – where trees (whether planted or established naturally) had previously belonged automatically to landlords, not crofting tenants. Crofters in Borve and Annishader, two townships just north of Portree, Skye's principal settlement, were among the pioneers of crofting forestry. Before planting could start on their grazings, however, they needed the consent of their landlord, Major John Macdonald of Tote, owner of one of Skye's smaller estates. Obtaining the necessary consent proved 'difficult', Borve crofter Alaistar Nicolson recalls – until, Nicolson continues, 'the landlord suggested we should simply buy him out'. At a meeting of Borve and Annishader crofters on 8 February 1993, it was accordingly agreed that the crofters should set up a trust, Borve and Annishader Township Ltd, which would try to take the two townships and their grazings – some 4,500 acres in all – into community ownership.

Supposing the success of the Assynt people in securing the North Lochinver Estate turns out to be an isolated triumph, it will be immensely worthwhile in itself ... But of course the intense hope must be that North Lochinver Estate is not a one-off but a trail-blazer; that the inspiration which has been provided by the splendid people who have conducted this campaign will now set a whole movement rolling ... The precise possibilities cannot be prescribed, but I have no doubt that they will unfold. North Lochinver Estate will become the new model for the future. Others will aspire to it, and ways will be found to meet that aspiration.

Brian Wilson MP, (Labour: Cunninghame North), December 1992: **West Highland Free Press,** *11 December 1992.*

Crofters at Borve in Skye were the first to follow Assynt's example and go for community ownership.

Highland cattle at Borve.

Since no open-market sale was envisaged, since all the land involved was under crofting tenure, and since John Macdonald (greatly to his credit) was willing to accept a price calculated more or less in accordance with the 1976 Crofting Reform Act formula for fixing the price of individual crofts, the cost of taking Borve and Annishader into community ownership was just £20,000. Of this sum, £7,000 was contributed upfront by the twenty or so crofters involved; a £5,000 grant came from Skye and Lochalsh Enterprise, HIE's local offshoot; and a low-interest loan of £8,000 was made available by the Highland Fund, a charity which had been assisting small-scale development in the Highlands and Islands since the 1950s. With next to no difficulty, then, Borve and Annishader followed the North Lochinver Estate into community ownership.

'Our first priority was to pay off our Highland Fund loan,' Alaistar Nicolson comments. 'Next we set about our crofting forestry scheme. Eventually, we carried out three such schemes. But the best thing about community ownership, as far as we've been concerned, is that – from the first – it made people think seriously about crofting possibilities that might not otherwise have been considered. As a result, a number of crofts changed hands – from father to son – in ways that got young people actively involved in land management. That's helped greatly with the various agricultural and other developments we're still pushing on with.'

When, in August 1995, Conservative MP Michael Forsyth became Secretary of State for Scotland, he made known that he would be interested in hearing from anyone with innovative ideas about policies he might pursue. This book's author, taking the Scottish Secretary at his word, wrote to him to suggest that the cause of community ownership – because it fostered self-reliance, enterprise and associated virtues – was one he ought to back. On 16 October, at a meeting with me in Skye where I then lived, Michael Forsyth rejected out of hand any thought of his 'expropriating', as he put it, private landlords. But he was by no means averse, he made clear, to encouraging such landlords to think about voluntary sales, on the Borve and Annishader model, to crofting trusts. And despite the earlier failure of Russell Sanderson's similar initiative, Michael Forsyth, it became evident, was intent on doing what he could to bring about community ownership of state-owned land.

No matter what your politics, it is no small honour that the Secretary of State for Scotland would see fit to visit us here in Assynt. I'm hopeful that this visit may be seen as endorsement of the idea of crofters taking control over their land.

Allan MacRae, Assynt Crofters Trust, October 1995: **Am Bratach, November 1995.**

The transfer of power and responsibility to local communities is a key plank in the [Conservative] government's philosophy, and the crofters in Assynt are to be congratulated for their pioneering efforts in setting up a crofting trust.

Michael Forsyth, Secretary of State for Scotland, October 1995: **West Highland Free Press, 27 October 1995.**

On 20 October 1995, Michael Forsyth visited Assynt and met with representatives of the Assynt Crofters Trust. 'What I want to know,' he said to them, 'is whether you have found ownership has made a real difference and, if it has, can we do what you did ten times over?' At an Inverness press conference that same day, the Secretary of State, having first assured the media (perhaps a little superfluously) that he was 'no Bolshevik', commented: 'I am not in the business of taking people's land away from them … [But] I am keen to encourage all crofters and crofting landlords to consider the crofting trust option and, as Secretary of State, I am interested in transferring ownership of the substantial crofting lands I hold to crofting or community trusts if there is sufficient interest at local level.'

One immediate consequence of Michael Forsyth's advocacy of community ownership was the emergence in December 1995 of the Crofting Trust Advisory Service (CTAS). Established by Highlands and Islands Enterprise in partnership with the Crofters Commission, the official body dealing with crofting regulation, CTAS had the job of helping groups of crofters interested in doing what had already been done by their counterparts in Assynt, Borve and Annishader. Among the first crofters to benefit from CTAS assistance were tenants on the Hope and Melness Estate on the north coast of Sutherland. Towards the end of 1995, their landlord, Michael Foljambe, who lived in Nottinghamshire and whose family had owned the property since 1952, indicated – in a gesture which anticipated Fred Taylor's cost-free transfer of Scalpay to its residents – that he was prepared to make over all the crofting land on his estate, without charge, to its tenants. Six townships and some seventy households were involved. Within weeks, agreement had been reached, and a further 10,800 acres – extending for five miles along the shoreline of the Kyle of Tongue – was in community control.

It has always saddened me that children have to leave Melness as soon as they finish their schooling. There is no possibility of me living there, and I think that the local community could develop its possibilities better than I can from afar … I believe that crofters have the right to make their own decisions … Neither finance nor politics come into this … I just want the young people to be able to stay in the area.

Michael Foljambe, owner of the Hope and Melness Estate, November 1995: John MacAskill, **We Have Won the Land: The Story of the Purchase by the Assynt Crofters Trust of the North Lochinver Estate,** *Acair, 1999.*

There are now three local, democratically-elected and accountable land trusts in the Highlands: the Stornoway Trust, which has operated successfully since the 1920s, the [North] Assynt Trust in [Sutherland] and the Borve [and Annishader] Trust in Skye. These trusts will act as an inspiration and a model which other communities will wish in time to follow … The initiative has to come from local people, but when it does the government should assist financially and administratively. Step by step, estate by estate, such community initiatives could change the face of Scotland.

Calum Macdonald MP, (Labour: Western Isles), March 1995: West Highland Free Press, 24 March 1995.

Michael Forsyth, meanwhile, was exploring the possibility of extending the community ownership principle to land in Forestry Commission hands. It had been drawn to his attention that, for some years, people living in Laggan, a locality west of Newtonmore in the Central Highlands, had been trying to get control of the commission's 3,500 acre Strathmashie Forest – which had once provided more than thirty Laggan residents with jobs but which, by the 1990s, had ceased to be a source of local employment. The Laggan Forest Trust, a group of Laggan residents, wanted to remedy that by taking over management of Strathmashie. This was something the Forestry Commission, despite repeated lobbying, refused to countenance until Michael Forsyth, having visited Laggan and met with trust representatives, instructed the commission to change tack. The Forestry Commission's then director-general, David Bills, duly took personal responsibility for matters at Laggan. Purchase of Strathmashie Forest by the local community proved impossible – because of the very high value attaching to several thousand acres of mature woodland. But the Laggan Forest Trust and the Forestry Commission, it was agreed, should jointly constitute a Laggan Forest Partnership in which local interests would have a meaningful say. The partnership thus established has since been a substantial influence on forest management in the Laggan area.

'Our original aim was to get ownership of Strathmashie Forest in its entirety,' says Laggan Forest Trust chairman, Rory Richardson. 'We weren't able to achieve that in the 1990s. But it's an aspiration we've never given up on and, indeed, it's one that's now firmly on our agenda. In the first instance, we might look to lease woodland from the

Welcome to Strathmashie Forest: A Community Forest: A Partnership between Laggan Forest Trust and the Forestry Commission.

Signboard, Strathmashie Forest, July 2011.

Join the pack at Laggan Wolftrax! Opened in 2005, Laggan Wolftrax is an exciting, purpose-built singletrack mountainbike centre for all-year-round use. Guaranteed to leave you panting for more! Drink in the stunning views of Loch Laggan, the hill fort at Dun na Lamh, and the natural beauty of Strathmashie – which you'll see from whichever route you ride – and you're guaranteed to understand why Laggan Wolftrax is something special! Dare to try the purpose-built, testing singletrack, and the unique experience is complete! So, fantastic, exciting trails, new quality bikes for hire, bike wash, changing and shower facilities, a top-notch on-site café serving home-made food and a cool, relaxing atmosphere!

Laggan Wolftrax welcome leaflet, July 2011.

Forestry Commission. But our ideal is to be fully in control. Although we'd admit to having made mistakes along the way, we've learned a lot in the last fifteen years about what's involved in forest management, and we believe we now have the capacity to be in sole charge.'

Among lessons learned by the Laggan Forest Trust, Richardson says, is the importance of developing woodland-based income sources other than those deriving from timber sales. Hence his stress on the benefits accruing from the construction in Strathmashie Forest of the elaborate set of mountain-bike trails known as Laggan Wolftrax. These trails now attract some 30,000 visitors annually – injecting £500,000 or more each year into a local economy which has been boosted hugely by the trade thus generated for hotels, bed-and-breakfast establishments, Laggan's village store and other businesses. 'We've helped create several jobs,' Rory Richardson goes on.

Thousands of acres of plantation forestry have been brought into community ownership in the Highlands and Islands – among them this piece of woodland in Knoydart.

'We've got houses that were empty into local occupation. We've helped make Wolftrax a success. But there's much still to do. We're looking to develop better camping and caravanning facilities, create some sort of adventure centre in the forest, make better training opportunities available to local youngsters. None of this might be totally dependent on bringing Strathmashie into community ownership. But we believe the returns to the locality from all these activities will be greater if we, and not the commission, own the forest.'

Michael Forsyth's 1995 intervention in the Strathmashie Forest saga transformed attitudes in Forestry Commission Scotland (FCS) and opened the way for what eventually became known as the National Forest Land Scheme – the means by which FCS today enables communities to buy or lease forest land for a range of purposes. Dozens of community-owned woodlands have resulted from this initiative. One of the largest belongs to the North West Mull Community Woodland Company (NWMCWC).

In the five years since taking over some 1,700 acres of established plantations from the Forestry Commission, NWMCWC has achieved a great deal. 'The biggest project we've completed has involved the construction of ten miles of road and four bridges,' comments the company's development manager, Ian Hepburn. 'That will make it possible for us to fell and extract some 80,000 tons of timber over the next two years – with another 50,000 tons to follow in the year or two after that.'

Timber sales will boost NWMCWC's cash flow – as will the micro-hydro scheme the company is planning to put in place. Plans for affordable housing, both for sale and for rent, are well advanced – as is the provision of a number of woodland crofts. Such crofts – whose occupants would combine agricultural activities with forest management in a way long common in Scandinavia but practically unknown in Scotland – have been talked about for several years. But the three woodland crofts which NWMCWC is establishing during 2011, and the further six such smallholdings which will follow, are the first to have got beyond the discussion stage. Together, says Ian Hepburn, its crofting and housing ventures will add up to

National Forest Land [consists of] the forests, woods, open land and other property owned by Scottish ministers on behalf of the nation, and managed by Forestry Commission Scotland. The National Forest Land Scheme gives community organisations, recognised non-governmental organisations (NGOs), and/or appropriate housing bodies the opportunity to buy or lease National Forest Land where they can provide increased public benefits.

Forestry Commission Scotland website, July 2011.

North West Mull Community Woodland Company is a community company with charitable status set up to manage Langamull and West Ardhu woodlands in the north west of the Isle of Mull. These woodlands were purchased through the National Forest Land Scheme from Forestry Commission Scotland in 2006 … Community benefits will include the provision of affordable housing, improved access, business opportunities and the use of the woodlands as an education resource.

NWMCWC website, June 2011.

a substantial community woodland company contribution to providing homes and livelihoods on an island where – after many decades of population decline – more and more people are looking to move in.

A similar commitment to boosting island prospects is evident on the part of Bute Community Land Company which, in July 2010, bought a large slice of Rhubodach Forest at the north end of Bute, one of the Clyde islands, from its previous owner, film director Richard Attenborough. Originally, the company hoped to buy all of Lord Attenborough's 1,700 acres of commercial woodland – but had to settle for 400 acres plus a right to develop footpaths, cycle tracks and other projects in the remainder. 'We want to make Bute Community Land Company self-sufficient financially,' says company director Jim Mitchell. 'It's early days and we've a long way to go. But on an island where there's been a lot of economic difficulty and a good deal of social deprivation, we feel we can help rebuild people's confidence.'

Few community-owned woodlands are as extensive as those managed by the North West Mull Community Woodland Company or its Bute counterpart. And many of the smaller woodlands now in community control have been acquired in order to enhance

The essence of woodland crofts would be to link housing, local rural livelihoods and woodland management. Woodland could bring new business dimensions to crofting activity and enable ... rural development to be realised.

Forestry Commission Scotland, **The Potential and Practicalities of Forest Crofts,** *January 2006.*

Rhubodach Forest is an area of ancient woodland, commercial forest, moorland and coast on the Isle of Bute. In July 2010 Bute Community Land Company (a charitable company owned by the residents of the island) purchased 161 hectares of forest and acquired rights over a further 535 hectares for footpaths, cycle paths and hydro schemes. Right from the start, the purchase of the forest was seen as the first important step in the community taking charge of its own destiny and leading the social and economic regeneration of the island.

Bute Forest website, 2011.

I am so proud of the Bute Community Land Company and the local people who have made this all happen. They have shown enormous perseverance, imagination, energy and resilience to get this result, and they will not stop now. They have started a process and unleashed new levels of confidence that are now unstoppable, and will deliver real benefits for Bute and its people.

Jim Mather, Scottish Government Enterprise Minister, July 2010: Bute Community Land Company press release, 28 July 2010.

or preserve local amenity rather than with a view to engaging in developmental effort of the type occurring in North West Mull – the type envisaged too by the Laggan Forest Trust. Partly for this reason, there has always been more interest, from the community side, in purchasing bits and pieces of woodland than there has been in taking control of the government-owned crofting estates which Michael Forsyth, like Russell Sanderson, was convinced (rightly in this writer's opinion) could readily be run better, and more constructively, by their residents than by the various bureaucracies which have managed them for the last eighty or more years.

In February 1996, stressing that the emergence of crofting trusts in Assynt and elsewhere had proved that 'local communities can take effective control of their own affairs', Michael Forsyth launched a consultative process which culminated, just over a year later, in the Transfer of Crofting Estates Act, the first land-reforming legislation of the modern era. Intended to facilitate the transfer of state-controlled croft land to this land's occupants, the Act failed for a long time to bring about any such transfers. Although this was partly because many of the government's crofting tenants – as had been discovered in Skye and Raasay at the start of the 1990s – were inherently reluctant to opt for community ownership, it was also a consequence of obstacles encountered by crofters, such as those occupying the government's 27,000 acre Keoldale Estate in Sutherland, who were eager to take advantage of the Transfer of Crofting Estates Act's provisions. Both before and during the Act's passage through parliament, Michael Forsyth and other Ministers indicated that government-owned crofting estates might be made over to their residents 'free of charge'. Within weeks of the Transfer of Crofting Estates Act having become law in March 1997, however, the Conservative government lost office. Subsequent administrations were to insist that state-owned assets, crofting estates included, could only be disposed of at market price. This, more than anything else, explains why the Transfer of Crofting Estates Act had been on the statute book for more than ten years before a group of crofters succeeded in taking charge of one of the localities the Act was meant to ease into community control.

Those crofters live on the Atlantic coast of South Harris and occupy one of the most scenically spectacular localities in the British Isles – a place where wide expanses of

I was surprised to find when I became Secretary of State for Scotland last summer that I was the largest crofting landlord in Scotland ... It seemed to me that there was an opportunity to launch a new initiative which would help to give crofters more effective control over their land. We surely need to ask whether these estates would not be better run in the future by local communities themselves rather than [by] a government department which, with the best will in the world, cannot be as sensitive to a community's needs and priorities as those who actually live there. The aim of the crofting trust initiative is to ensure that the day to day management of estates, and the use of the land, is sympathetic to local needs. Ownership of the land will also allow the local crofting community to exploit potential development opportunities in both the short and long term. Our initiative provides a valuable opportunity for crofters, on those estates for which I have responsibility, to attain ownership and control of the land they work ... And let me make one thing absolutely clear. We are not disposing of these estates in order to raise money for the Exchequer. We are opening this window of opportunity for the crofting communities because it is the right thing to do. It is a matter of principle … Such is our commitment to this cause that we are even prepared, if the circumstances justify it, to transfer certain crofts free of charge … Our aim is to make sure that crofting trusts get off to a good start and succeed. And … the terms of transfer will reflect this.

Michael Forsyth, Secretary of State for Scotland, addressing a meeting of the House of Commons' Scottish Grand Committee in Inverness, on 5 February 1996.

An Act to enable the Secretary of State to dispose of his crofting estates and certain other property of his in the crofting counties to approved crofting bodies.

Preamble, **Transfer of Crofting Estates (Scotland) Act, 1997.**

natural grassland (called *machair* in Gaelic) border white shell-sand beaches and (when the sun shines) startlingly turquoise seas. In contrast to its eastern shoreline, which is rocky and infertile, South Harris's 'west side', as the district is called by islanders, is agriculturally desirable. The area was accordingly turned over to sheep farmers in the 1820s – when scores of evicted families were relocated to their island's comparatively barren east coast or, in many cases, shipped to Nova Scotia. About a hundred years later, however, the public agency that subsequently evolved into DAFS took ownership of three west side properties, Luskentyre, Borve and Scaristavore, with the aim of re-establishing them as crofting settlements. The late Finlay J Macdonald, a broadcaster and author who grew up on one of the crofts that then took shape on Scaristavore, the most southerly of the west side's three government-owned estates, long afterwards recalled the new community as a place of 'spiritual and physical magic'. But as Scaristavore's settlers – Macdonald's parents among them – were to discover, Harris, for much of the twentieth century, offered little in the way of income beyond the usually meagre returns to be got from a modestly sized croft. In the fifty years to 2001, the island's population halved. At the start of the twenty-first century, moreover, more than a third of the people still living on the government's Scaristavore, Borve and Luskentyre estates were over 65. Where there had once been three primary schools, there was just one, at Seilebost, and it was threatened with closure on the grounds that, by 2007, the west side of Harris, where Finlay J Macdonald had been one youngster among many, contained only fifteen school-age children – and just a single pre-school child.

In 1919 a host of island soldiers and sailors had returned from the First World War eager to make a new start and get for themselves a share of the 'land fit for heroes to live in' which … someone in the elevated realms of government had promised them … My father and seven others were lucky … A large and lush estate on the Atlantic coast of Harris was … divided and rented out as eight crofts [by the then Department of Agriculture for Scotland] … For me the new village wove a spiritual and physical magic as I grew up with it. It was carved out from what had been the granary of the Clan MacLeod in the days of that clanship. The Atlantic thundered or shimmied according to its mood on mile upon mile of shell-white beach which, in turn, was selvedge to rolling green meadowland [or] … *machair* as it was called in Gaelic … And the whole panorama was contained in a crescent swathe of tall mountains whose names … bore testimony to the Viking occupation of those lands a thousand years before. If it all sounds idyllic, it's because it was to the boy who was I.

Finlay J Macdonald, **Crowdie and Cream, Futura, 1983.**

That child's father, Neil Campbell, is a chartered accountant and business adviser who, with his wife Rhoda, operates an award-winning tourism business based on the purpose-built and imaginatively-designed holiday cottages the couple have developed on their croft at Scarista. A longstanding advocate of community ownership, Neil was involved from the outset in the complex process – extending over several years – which culminated, towards the end of January 2010, in the Luskentyre, Borve and Scaristavore estates being formally handed over to their tenants and residents by the Scottish government's Environment Minister, Roseanna Cunningham. 'What motivated myself and others from the outset is our need to have more young people setting up home here,' Neil Campbell says. 'One of our basic aims is to make house sites available at a well-below-market-value price to families who'll live here all the year round. That will help retain our primary school and other vital services. The alternative, sooner rather than later, is the extinction of viable community life on the west side of Harris.'

Harris has an ageing and declining population with too few people in the economically important 16–44 age group. In order to attempt to redress that balance a community with greater economic opportunities and wider social provision needs to be created which is attractive to an increasing number of young people and their families.

West Harris Trust, **Business Plan**, *October 2009.*

West Harris Trust board members, left to right, Murdo MacKay (the trust's chairman), Rhoda MacDonald, Fiona MacLennan and Neil Campbell.

I was born and brought up on the Isle of Skye. Following my marriage to Rhoda in 2001, we decided to settle on her family croft in Scaristavore [in Harris] where we have developed luxury self-catering accommodation … We have two children, Rachel who is in primary three at Seilebost school and Angus, aged four, who has the 'distinction' of being the only pre-school child resident on the west side of Harris … I have believed in the value of a community owned trust for several years … I am particularly keen to see additional young families settle in the community to ensure that my son Angus has friends and classmates when he starts school next year.

Neil Campbell, West Harris Trust website, February 2011.

While local discussion about what might be done to improve the west side's long-term prospects began much earlier, the first substantial step along the road to community ownership was taken in January 2007 when, following a well-attended public meeting in Seilebost School, a steering group whose members included Neil Campbell was given the job of mapping possible ways forward. One of the group's key recommendations – that the Scaristavore, Borve and Luskentyre estates be got into community ownership – was endorsed in a subsequent postal ballot by a large majority on a turn-out of no less than 94 per cent. But for all the public backing it enjoyed, the West Harris Trust, constituted in 2008 with a view to taking control of the state-owned croft land on Harris's Atlantic coast, faced an uphill task. The establishment of a devolved Scottish government in 1999 had resulted in responsibility for such land being transferred to this government by the Westminster-based ministers who had previously been in charge of it. But the SNP administration which took power in Edinburgh in 2007 – the administration with which the West Harris Trust had to negotiate – considered itself bound by Treasury Rules which, Scottish ministers insisted, made it impossible to dispose of assets such as their West Harris estates on the cost-free or knock-down basis envisaged when Michael Forsyth framed the legislation intended to make such disposals possible. Getting round that difficulty – a difficulty to which this book returns in conclusion – took the better part of two years. But eventually, on 25 January 2010, by which point the West Harris Trust's fund-raising efforts had been boosted by substantial grant aid from Highlands and Islands Enterprise and Comhairle nan Eilean Siar (the Western Isles Council), the Scottish government's Luskentyre, Borve and Scaristavore estates were taken over by their residents.

The West Harris Trust takes over the 4,500-acre estates of Borve, Luskentyre and Scaristavore on Monday. The crofters are the first to buy land owned by the state under legislation introduced a decade ago by the then Scottish Secretary Michael Forsyth. It is now hoped projects to build new homes and crofts, create jobs and develop small-scale renewables projects will encourage more people to live on the island and reverse the trend of depopulation. West Harris Trust secretary Neil Campbell said: 'Left to its own devices, the west side of Harris will continue a slow decline where the population will become more elderly and houses that become vacant will be bought for holiday homes. We want to address that.'

Scotsman, 19 January 2010.

Surfboarding on Harris's Atlantic coast.

West Harris is a very special place. Its spectacular beaches, its flower rich machair and its local culture make it a much sought after holiday location and a very enviable place to live. It is a wonderful place for children to grow up in and an ideal location for families. The West Harris Trust has been formed to inject life back into the area … The West Harris Trust will identify ten house sites within the area, and these will be made available for sale at an affordable price to families wishing to move into the area to live and work.

West Harris Trust website, February 2011.

The West Harris Trust was formed in 2008 to take ownership of the West Harris Estates from the Scottish Government. The trust is governed by social and community benefit considerations … West Harris has experienced significant population decline over the past several decades, with a 50 per cent population loss since 1951. This decline has been especially marked in the number of young families … One of the primary aims of the trust is to strengthen the community by attracting new families into the area. The trust, in partnership with local [crofter common] grazings committees, will offer house sites for sale at a significant discount to the current market value … The trust believes Seilebost School is central to our plans of re-generating the area; to this end priority will be given to families with young children committed to placing their children in this school.

West Harris Trust, Allocations Policy for Subsidised House Sites, May 2011.

The hill burn or stream where the North Harris Trust are planning a small-scale hydro development.

Twenty years had passed since Russell Sanderson first offered DAFS tenants in Skye and Raasay the chance to do what was thus accomplished in Harris. Much had changed in the interim. Above all, it had been shown that community ownership – notwithstanding the apprehensions which led to the rejection of the Sanderson proposal – could open the way to achieving social and economic renewal of the sort the West Harris Trust was looking to bring about. Luskentyre, Borve and Scaristavore residents wanted to expand the west side of Harris's dwindling population by creating new housing opportunities, developing small-scale renewables ventures and otherwise capitalising on the potential of the various assets they had acquired. To figure out how their agenda might be delivered, they needed only to draw on the experience of some of their Hebridean neighbours – prominent among them people living on the island of Eigg.

Inverie, Knoydart's principal settlement.

4

WE JUST WANT TO BUY A LITTLE SECURITY

Isle of Eigg Heritage Trust
Community Land Unit
Knoydart Foundation
Land Reform Policy Group
Orbost Estate

The Isle of Eigg is one of the most beautiful Hebridean Islands, lying ten miles off the Scottish west coast, south of the Isle of Skye. The island has a fascinating history, superb wildlife and a vibrant community. Whether you come to climb Britain's largest pitchstone ridge, watch eagles over stunning white beaches, learn about the world's first fully renewably powered electricity grid, mix with the locals at a ceilidh dance, or simply to relax away from the pressures of modern life, you are sure to enjoy your stay on Eigg and return again and again.

Isle of Eigg website, July 2011.

CHAPTER FOUR

We just want to buy a little security

Isle of Eigg Heritage Trust § Community Land Unit § Knoydart Foundation
Land Reform Policy Group § Orbost Estate

Eigg Electric's wind turbines, with the Sgurr in the background.

Served by a year-round but not always daily ferry from the nearby mainland settlement of Mallaig, sixteen miles away, the 7,500 acre island of Eigg is one of the Small Isles – the others being Muck, Rum and Canna – strung out across the patch of ocean lying between Skye (to the north) and Ardnamurchan (part of the Highland mainland). Described by the Scottish Wildlife Trust – a conservation charity which has had a long association with the island – as 'exceptionally diverse' environmentally, Eigg has always been an attractive place to visit. For much of the last quarter of the twentieth century, however, it was not a pleasant place to live – many of its troubles being attributed, by islanders and others, to the nature of the island's ownership.

In 1828, when the MacDonalds of Clanranald, clan chieftains who had been in control of Eigg and adjacent localities since the middle ages, were following lots of other such chieftains into bankruptcy, the island was sold to the first of a long succession of non-resident lairds. Few of them retained Eigg for long – an exception being the Runciman family whose wealth derived from their shipping interests and who were Eigg's landlords from 1925 until 1966. The Runcimans, much the most warmly regarded of Eigg's twentieth-century proprietors, were succeeded by a Welsh farmer, Robert Evans, who, after just five years, sold the island to the Anglyn Trust. This was a supposedly charitable organisation headed by Bernard Farnham-Smith who described himself as a retired naval commander but who – or so it was stated in the course of an exchange in the House of Commons in February 1997 – had actually held no rank higher than that of 'a very junior officer in the London fire brigade'. When, three years after its purchase of Eigg, the Anglyn Trust, which had paid £90,000 for the island in 1971, put Eigg on the market for £200,000, there was some prospect – because of the difficulties resulting from repeated ownership changes – that Eigg would be bought by the Highlands and Islands Development Board. But the Anglyn Trust refused to sell to a public body, and Eigg was sold instead to a Yorkshire-based businessman, Keith Schellenberg, who immediately suggested to the HIDB that, since its interest in Eigg had raised the island's price, the board should give him a hefty grant by way of compensation.

Years later, following the collapse of the libel action he raised against the *Guardian* in response to that newspaper's coverage of Eigg's eventual acquisition by its residents, Schellenberg would be described as 'a Toad of Toad Hall character' to whom 'buying the island of Eigg must have felt like buying his own little kingdom in the Hebrides'. Initially, however, nothing of this was apparent. Indeed Eigg's latest proprietor seemed set on developing both the island's agricultural potential and its still greater potential as a tourist destination. Substantial sums were invested and new residents attracted – mostly to fill jobs Keith Schellenberg created. Among those incomers was Maggie

Eigg and the Highland mainland as viewed from the Sgurr, the island's highest point.

Eigg farmer Colin Carr who, with his family, was threatened with eviction by one of the island's last private landlords.

Fyffe who afterwards led Eigg's long march to community ownership but who, on her arrival with her husband Wes in 1976, began by being grateful to Eigg's laird for having given her and Wes the opportunity, as Maggie put it subsequently, 'to live in such a beautiful place, to have a safe environment to bring up children, and to be part of a small community'. Marie Carr, who grew up on Eigg and who still lives there, was equally taken with the beginnings of the 'Schellenberg era', as islanders call the twenty or so years between the mid-1970s and the mid-1990s. 'I was sixteen when Keith Schellenberg bought Eigg,' Marie says. 'I thought he was fantastic. He was bringing in lots of new people. There was so much going on. It was all just absolutely great.'

This euphoria did not last. As the 1970s turned into the 1980s, investment started to falter, estate employees began to be laid off and so tight did money become that the landlord's locally resident farm manager found himself without diesel for his tractor. Estate workers who quit or were sacked, and who lost their tied houses as a result, were refused alternative accommodation. Homes rented to islanders – many of them elderly because Eigg's young people were leaving – deteriorated to a point where housing conditions on the island became something of a scandal. In the course of his failed libel proceedings against the *Guardian*, 'a picture was painted,' the newspaper reported, 'of islanders living in rat-infested hovels with leaking roofs and damp-filled walls. Anne Campbell, an old lady who lived on the island, described how she used to drown the rats she had caught in her house in the sink.' Making matters worse, or so the High Court in London was told, were the gratuitously offensive antics indulged in by the laird and his friends in the course of their summertime visits. When a Nazi banner was draped on one occasion from a window balcony at Eigg Lodge, his island home, this was, the court heard, by way of being a joke.

Last night islanders on Eigg were planning a huge party … to celebrate the final victory over the [island's] former owner who plagued their lives for more than twenty years. Throughout the five-week trial [resulting from Schellenberg's libel action against the *Guardian*] a picture emerged of Keith Schellenberg as a Toad of Toad Hall character. It was an apt analogy: [Eigg's laird] racing around the island in his Rolls Royce, wearing a tweed jacket and goggles, his scarf flapping in the wind, and with little regard for anybody else. No doubt in his own mind the islanders of Eigg are the weasels and stoats who drove him from the Lodge, Eigg's version of Toad Hall. But yesterday there was no kindly Mole or Badger to save Mr Schellenberg from the ignominy of his High Court defeat. A millionaire playboy who made his money in the motor industry, shipbuilding, livestock feed and agricultural chemicals, Mr Schellenberg is a larger than life character. He bobsleighed in the Winter Olympics, regularly careered down the Cresta Run, and raced power boats. For Mr Schellenberg, buying the island of Eigg must have felt like buying his own little kingdom in the Hebrides. But as islanders who made the two-day journey from Eigg to Court 13 of the High Court [in London] testified, Scotland's feudal landlord system granted the laird power over virtually all aspects of their lives. Employment, housing, maintenance, transport, the island's communal buildings: nothing could be done on the estate without Mr Schellenberg's say-so.

Guardian, 20 May 1999.

Among the causes of Eigg's mounting problems were the terms of its laird's divorce in 1980 from his second wife, Margaret de Hauteville Udny-Hamilton, a member of an Aberdeenshire landowning family. Because she had contributed half of the price paid for Eigg in 1975, Ms Udny-Hamilton, afterwards Mrs Margaret Williams, retained a 50 per cent stake in the island – a peculiar arrangement that led to management becoming a process of negotiation between the former couple or their legal representatives. Eventually, in 1989, by which point Schellenberg's share of Eigg had been vested in one of his companies, Mrs Williams took legal action in order to force her ex-husband to sell the island – her aim being to establish the cash value of her ownership stake which she now wished to realise. Court proceedings lasted for more than two years – the resulting uncertainty causing matters on Eigg to become even more chaotic.

'There are only two things growing on Eigg,' Torcuil Crichton of the *West Highland Free Press* reported from Eigg as the Williams-Schellenberg dispute was getting underway, 'bracken and the rabbit population. Everything else is stagnant, breaking down or already broken down … The general air is one of decay.' Dr Hector McLean, Eigg's veteran GP, then 77, was more forceful. 'The island has gone to the dogs,' he declared. This was also the opinion of another much younger and mainland-based GP, Dr Michael Foxley, who had been elected to Highland Regional Council in 1986 and whose council ward included the Small Isles. One of the radically-inclined

The island has gone to the dogs … I was told a long time before he came here that the last thing a Hebridean island needed was an international playboy. It seems to me that Eigg is just another of Schellenberg's toys, like his cars and his boats.

Dr Hector McLean, Small Isles GP, August 1989: West Highland Free Press, 11 August 1989.

councillors who were beginning to make their voices heard during this period in the Highlands and Islands, Michael Foxley was shocked by the conditions he discovered on Eigg. If Eigg was again put up for sale, he announced in August 1989, he would 'formally ask' the regional council 'to purchase the island'.

Although Highland Regional Council (or Highland Council as the local authority was renamed in 1995) would – thanks to Michael Foxley's constant promptings – become more and more engaged with Eigg as the 1990s advanced, the council was unwilling, on its becoming evident during 1991 that a further sale of the island was imminent, to contemplate taking sole control. But alternatives to private ownership – perhaps involving the council acting in collaboration with other organisations and with islanders themselves – began to be talked about. They were talked about more widely when, in the summer of 1991, an Isle of Eigg Trust was formed with the aim of raising the cash needed to buy the island. Constituted by four of Eigg's mainland well-wishers, the most prominent of whom was academic and ecological activist Alastair McIntosh, the trust started less promisingly than it might have done because of its founders having launched their initiative without prior consultation with islanders. This was remedied at a public meeting on Eigg in October 1991 when the concept of trust ownership – although somewhat undefined at this stage – attracted general backing. But in the circumstances of the time, with Assynt crofters' purchase of the North Lochinver Estate still in the future, the Eigg Trust's fund-raising efforts were not immediately fruitful. And even if they had been, Keith Schellenberg would not have been party to any sale to Alastair McIntosh and his colleagues. Speaking to the press in November 1991, he said of what the newly formed trust was trying to accomplish: 'It's got no basis in reality… It's the most gigantic soap opera of all time.'

When, following the failure of Schellenberg's efforts to prevent his ex-wife forcing a sale, the island was put on the market in May 1992 with an asking price of around £2 million, there were further attempts – promoted mainly by Michael Foxley – to engineer some sort of public-body-led purchase. But these attempts foundered on the refusal of the north of Scotland's principal source of development funding, Highlands and Islands Enterprise, to become involved. Just four weeks before the start of the

Assynt campaign that was to have the effect of modifying this attitude, an agency spokesman commented: 'We don't see how the purchase of Eigg could get straight financial assistance from HIE.' Less than a month later, it was announced that Keith Schellenberg had himself repurchased Eigg – having, in effect, bought out his former wife's half-share – and was now the island's sole owner.

This news left Eigg's people both demoralised and fearful. When journalist and broadcaster Lesley Riddoch, who was to become actively involved in the Eigg Trust, visited the island in July 1992 to make a radio programme about the place, the only local resident prepared to speak on air was now-retired doctor, Hector MacLean, who said that to live on Keith Schellenberg's Eigg was 'like living under enemy occupation'.

But inspired in part by events in Assynt, islanders became steadily more outspoken and increasingly willing to make clear to the media and others that, should Eigg once more come on the market, they would certainly try – with such external help as might be available – to make themselves the island's owners. The Eigg Residents Association, set up some years previously in order to give islanders a voice, now began to articulate this aspiration more and more forcefully – the association's chosen, and highly persuasive, spokesperson being Maggie Fyffe who, in the course of 1994, began to gain something of a national profile in Scotland.

That year had begun badly in Eigg when, at the start of January, the shed in which Keith Schellenberg stored the Rolls Royce he used when on the island caught fire and was burned out. The laird suspected sabotage on the part of people he dismissed, in comments to the press, as incoming 'hippies and drop-outs' who allegedly spent most of their time organising what he called 'acid-rock parties'. But police inquiries failed to substantiate Schellenberg's suspicions about the January fire, and Eigg's long-established residents, outraged by their landlord's comments about their more recently-arrived neighbours, issued a powerful statement intended both to underline the community's cohesion and 'to refute utterly the ludicrous allegations' directed by their laird at their more recently-arrived neighbours.

[It's] like living under enemy occupation … except that you're not allowed to shoot the buggers.

Dr Hector MacLean on life on Eigg during the Schellenberg era, July 1992: Alastair McIntosh, 'Colonised Land, Colonised Mind', Resurgence, No 184, 1997.

The one thing which did lift our spirits that year [1992] was the news that the Assynt Crofters Trust had been successful in their bid to buy their land. This was undoubtedly a turning point, not only for the people of Eigg but for many other communities across the Highlands.

Maggie Fyffe, reflecting on Eigg's route to community ownership, December 1997: Personal memo shared with the author.

We who have been born and brought up on the island would like to refute utterly the ludicrous allegations [made] about the community here. The island has a small but united population of local families and incomers who are between them struggling to develop a community with a long-term future against the apparent wishes of an owner who seems to want us to live in primitive conditions … If the nature of the island has changed, it could be something to do with the fact that all the local men working for the estate during Schellenberg's first years have left, taking their indigenous way of life with them. The incoming islanders play an active, caring part in the community. They help run the senior citizens' lunch club, they drive the community minibus to enable those without transport to get to the shop or church, and they have organised a Gaelic playgroup so that their children will have a chance of learning Gaelic in order to preserve the traditional culture of the island.

Statement issued by Eigg's indigenous population, January 1994.

In February, the BBC were back on Eigg to record a further radio programme, this one in the shape of a debate featuring both the island's laird and Allan MacRae of the Assynt Crofters Trust 'I can see the proprietor here has no conscience or commitment as far as the people here are concerned,' Allan said. 'I think the people here have to take the initiative themselves … People can shape the future if they have a will to do it.' This advice, from a man who had certainly practised what he preached, began to be acted on. A group of islanders got together to explore how community ownership might be made a reality. Michael Foxley remained supportive. The Scottish Wildlife Trust, which had had a presence on Eigg since the 1970s, made public its wish to be involved in a future purchase of the island. And the Eigg Trust was reconstituted – with the bulk of its now eight trustees being locally-elected Eigg residents. The people involved in these various endeavours, Keith Schellenberg commented, were 'dangerous', 'rotten', 'barmy revolutionaries'. But when, in October, he began to issue eviction notices, one

Maggie Fyffe (right) with fellow islander and local historian, Camille Dressler. Maggie was central to the drive for community ownership of Eigg.

of which was intended to lead to the removal of Marie Carr, her husband Colin and their five children from their farmhouse home, his position became so untenable that Eigg's proprietor decided, as he would subsequently tell a Yorkshire newspaper, that he had had enough of 'trying to tame the Scots'. In March 1995 Eigg duly experienced its sixth change of owner in just thirty years when it was announced that Keith Schellenberg had sold the island privately, for some £1.6 million, to a German artist, Marlin Eckhart, who preferred to be known as Maruma – a name, it was reported, he had adopted on discerning its shape while gazing into a pool of water in Abu Dhabi.

That Maruma was an eccentric was evident from the first – it being his self-proclaimed mission, he told journalists, to create 'pictures from the world beyond matter … [by means of] telepathic connection … with the materialised powers of fire'. That the artist was a financially hard-pressed eccentric became clear when it was revealed, first, that he had obtained a large loan secured against his ownership of Eigg and, second, that the island estate's few remaining employees were not receiving any wages. By July 1996, to no-one's astonishment, Eigg was on sale yet again – for £400,000 more than the £1.6 million purchase price of the year before.

This time, however, islanders and their allies were better organised than they had ever been. Some months previously, Michael Foxley, whose consistently outspoken support for community ownership earlier led to his being branded an 'extremist' by a fellow councillor in the course of a particularly heated council meeting, had succeeded in getting overwhelming backing for the proposition that Highland Council should, like the Scottish Wildlife Trust, line up behind the people of Eigg in their battle to obtain what Maggie Fyffe called 'just … a little security'. 'If we didn't help them, we would be neglecting our obligation to the people of the Highlands,' said Peter Peacock, now council convener. Soon a tripartite grouping – consisting of the Isle of Eigg Residents Association, the Scottish Wildlife Trust and Highland Council – had taken formal shape and secured the legal services of Simon Fraser who had done so much to help Assynt's crofters four years earlier. Named the Isle of Eigg Heritage Trust, the new body was up and running in time to commence formal fund-raising just weeks before Eigg became once more available for purchase.

The final straw came in October [1994] when Schellenberg issued two eviction notices – one to a local family with five children and the other to the resident wildlife warden … [This] turned out be the issue which totally united the community in its opposition to a system which could treat people with so little regard. The evictions never took place, but a feeling of insecurity and uncertainty affected everyone's life.

Maggie Fyffe reflecting on Eigg's route to community ownership, December 1997: Personal memo shared with the author.

People think … that when we say we want to buy the island we want power. They are wrong. We don't want to buy power; we just want to buy a little security.

Maggie Fyffe, February 1996: West Highland Free Press, 16 February 1996.

Eigg is on the conscience of the nation as perhaps the prime example of the negative aspects of current landownership patterns and practice. The islanders feel a deep sense of frustration at their inability to see their enterprise released.

Peter Peacock, Highland Council convener, August 1996: **West Highland Free Press, 2 August 1996.**

This is the best chance we will ever get to make a go of things on Eigg. We are thrilled with the public interest in our bid to buy the island and end the blight of absentee lairds.

Maggie Fyffe, August 1996: **West Highland Free Press, 30 August 1996.**

The interest in our appeal has been amazing. People from all over the country – and all over the world in some cases – have been contacting us and offering support.

Maggie Fyffe, September 1996: **West Highland Free Press, 6 September 1996.**

Frankly, I was rather appalled by the description [the residents] presented of an island whose infrastructure is crumbling and which is suffering from serious neglect. The present situation is pretty shocking and is not sustainable. The islanders have a right to a degree of security.

Michael Forsyth, Secretary of State to Scotland, on visiting Eigg, September 1996: **Herald, 26 September 1996.**

As had happened in the case of Assynt, there was an overwhelmingly positive response to Eigg people's appeal for the funds needed to buy the land on which they lived. But the sum required to get anywhere near Eigg's asking price was far greater than its Assynt equivalent had been. And there would be little help available, it was clear, from the public purse. Although Michael Forsyth visited Eigg in September 1996, where he declared himself 'appalled' by the 'pretty shocking' state of affairs he discovered, the Secretary of State for Scotland was not prepared to extend central government cash aid to the Isle of Eigg Heritage Trust. The trust, he indicated, should look to Highlands and Islands Enterprise for assistance. But for all that HIE's previous refusal to help get Eigg into alternative ownership was not now repeated, the development agency was by no means prepared to be generous. Comparing the Isle of Eigg Heritage Trust's endeavours to a building project, HIE's chief executive informed the media that, while his organisation was prepared to provide 'the last brick in the wall', it would be up to the trust to get the wall to a point where only one more brick was needed. Just how hard this was going to be became apparent when the Heritage Memorial Fund, one of the grant-giving bodies financed by Britain's then recently-established national lottery, turned down a request for assistance on the bizarre basis – as it appears in retrospect – that, if the Isle of Eigg Heritage Trust bid was successful, islanders would thereby be given too large a say in what was to happen on an island which, the Memorial Fund agreed, was of national significance environmentally. What saved the day, as it turned out, was the *Guardian* article – written by Scottish journalist Ruaridh Nicoll and entitled 'The Lairds of Misrule' – that was to lead to Keith Schellenberg's unsuccessful libel action against the newspaper. This article brought Eigg, a place she had never so much as visited, to the attention of a woman living in the north of England. This woman's identity has never been revealed. But on Eigg she is a heroine all the same – thanks to her having given the Isle of Eigg Heritage Trust no less than £750,000. Because the trust (being a registered charity) could reclaim a proportion of the taxes paid by donors, that gift boosted its funds by £1 million.

This was a remarkable development. But it was arguably no less remarkable than the Isle of Eigg Heritage Trust having already attracted several hundred thousand pounds in the form of small donations. There were thousands of these – every donor receiving a personal note of thanks from Maggie Fyffe. The money thus got together having been supplemented by a £17,000 grant from HIE and, more importantly, by the extraordinarily generous contribution made by that one anonymous well-wisher, the heritage trust was able – in a way that would not otherwise have been possible – to respond speedily when, in March 1997, one of Maruma's creditors enforced an immediate sale of the island. £1.5 million was offered for Eigg by the trust. At the beginning of April, this offer was accepted.

————

This is the day we have all dreamed about since we formed [our] partnership and set out on our journey … We have experienced many highs and also some lows along the way, but our resolve has never wavered and we are all overjoyed at the outcome. The public's response has been absolutely fantastic and makes us all the more determined to make a success of the way the island is run in the future.

Maggie Fyffe, April 1997: **West Highland Free Press, 11 April 1997.**

The inhabitants of Eigg finally took charge of their own destiny yesterday when they bought their island for £1.5m. The island, sold by Keith Schellenberg to German artist Maruma for £1.6m two years ago, has changed hands nine times since 1828. But now control has passed to the local community and their partners. Last night, their success in breaking the grip of private landlords on Eigg was being celebrated throughout Scotland as taking on the work begun in Assynt.

David Ross, **Herald, 5 April 1997.**

The main achievement [of the Isle of Eigg Heritage Trust] without a doubt is that, through the purchase [of Eigg by the trust], people have been able to stay on the island and have been able to provide economically for their families. The security of tenure issue was top in almost all responses [to a community survey] and it is clear that, in terms of housing, business opportunities and community activities, having security of tenure has been really important, and due recognition is given [by survey respondents] to the Trust for moving on this issue quickly and effectively.

Aigas Associates, **Isle of Eigg Heritage Trust: Independent Review, May 2007.**

One of my bed-and-breakfast guests last summer was a man who'd last been in Eigg a long time ago. He was amazed by what we've managed to do as a community, by what we've been able to achieve. He thought it was fantastic. A lot of my guests who knew Eigg in the past, and are now revisiting, say something similar. I like that.

Marie Carr, Eigg resident, in conversation with the author, June 2011.

Today Eigg is home to many more people than it was in 1997. A lot of them are young. Some, like Joe Cormack who makes a living from his music, grew up on Eigg. Others, like Jamie Ardagh, a Sussex graduate who combines crofting with a bike-hire business, are new arrivals. They and other islanders are beneficiaries of – and participants in – the work of the Isle of Eigg Heritage Trust. Its board consists of seven members. Four are elected by islanders; Highland Council and the Scottish Wildlife Trust (SWT) nominate one member each; and these six members appoint an independent chairman. Since 2007, this chairman has been John Hutchison.* Prior to his retirement, John was Highland Council's area manager for Lochaber, the council subdivision which includes the Small Isles – and, in this capacity, he had extensive dealings with Eigg both before and after the island's purchase by the trust he now heads. 'Much the biggest thing the Isle of Eigg Heritage Trust has done,' John Hutchison says, 'is to have given islanders self-respect and self-confidence.'

As demonstrated by the involvement of John Hutchison, SWT and Highland Council, the Isle of Eigg Heritage Trust differs markedly from the comparable body in Assynt – where crofters are in sole charge. However, Eigg people's external partners have always recognised that island interests take primacy over their own – and islanders, for their part, see advantages in having others involved in island affairs. Paradoxically, this has meant that islanders have come under pressure on occasion to end the partnership arrangement and take sole charge of Eigg. But this pressure, mostly from funding agencies, has been resisted. When, in 2007, Eigg residents were given the chance to opt for outright control, they accordingly preferred to stick with arrangements that had secured – and are still securing – all sorts of improvements.

One of the earliest of these, funded largely by HIE, was An Laimhrig, the name (in Gaelic it means The Harbour) given to the building visitors first reach on getting to Eigg from the mainland. An Laimhrig accommodates a restaurant, a shop, a craft shop, toilet and shower facilities (much used by the passing yacht crews who

---

* A declaration of interest. Between 2005 and 2007, I chaired the Isle of Eigg Heritage Trust, taking over from Simon Fraser, the trust's first chairman.

are a regular feature of the Eigg summer scene) and the Isle of Eigg Heritage Trust's headquarters – occupied most days by Maggie Fyffe who has been the trust's secretary since its inception. Opened on the first anniversary of the trust's 1997 purchase of the island, An Laimhrig was a significant advance in its own right. But it proved to be merely the initial component of an ongoing programme of social and economic renewal which has included: the refurbishment and modernisation of Eigg's community hall; the provision of long-term leases to tenants of trust-owned homes, farms and businesses; the upgrading of a number of houses and other buildings; the launch of a trust-owned construction company; the provision both of house-sites for sale and new homes for rent; the restructuring of croft land and the creation of new crofts; the establishment of a waste-collection service; the fencing and restocking of forestry plantations where the conifers planted by previous lairds are gradually giving way to wildlife-friendly trees of the kind that grew here in earlier times.

An Laimhrig, the Isle of Eigg Heritage Trust's first building project and now the island's social hub.

The Isle of Eigg Electrification Scheme is unique, in that ... it uses electrical energy derived from wind, sun and water, to power a high voltage distribution grid, which supplies electricity to all household and businesses in a small, scattered and isolated community with no input from the [British] National Grid. The output of renewable generators, hydro, wind or solar are very variable and, to guarantee 24-hour power, the system is supported by a bank of batteries, interacting directly with the grid through grid-connected inverters. When the batteries become discharged to a set degree, a back-up diesel generator is called in automatically, and mechanisms have been put in place to ensure that the generator and renewables, in particular the hydro, can run in phase together and each make their contribution to the recharging of the batteries.

The Institution of Engineering and Technology, in connection with a talk given to the institution by John Booth, December 2009.

A number of those developments are likely to feature when any Eigg resident is asked to list what has changed on Eigg since 1997. But top of everyone's list of what the Isle of Eigg Heritage Trust has accomplished is its construction of the electricty supply system run by a trust subsidiary, Eigg Electric. Because of the high cost that would have been involved in laying the necessary subsea cable, Eigg was never connected to Britain's national grid and islanders, as a result, depended for electricity on expensive and noisy diesel generators which, in most instances, they could afford to run for only a few hours each day. If Eigg was to have good prospects economically, the heritage trust was convinced from its inception, islanders had to have reliable, round-the-clock power of the type taken for granted practically everywhere else in the United Kingdom. Reaching this conclusion was easy. Working out how to provide the necessary electricity took longer. But by 2004 it had been agreed that the heritage trust should aim to connect every home, every business and every community facility on Eigg to a grid that would be, in effect, a miniature version of its Britain-wide counterpart. Because of the trust's commitment to combating climate change by reducing carbon dioxide emissions, this island grid would be required to deal for the most part in electricity generated from renewable sources. And since Eigg contained no single such source large or reliable enough to do the job, a mix of sources would have to be tapped. Thus it came about that, in February 2008, Eigg became the first community in the world to have its electricity needs met by integrating water power, wind power and solar power into one supply mechanism. Two diesel generators are available by way of emergency back-up. But with Eigg's so-called 'smart grid' obtaining some 92 per cent of its energy requirements from this grid's three renewable sources in the course of its first eighteen months, these have been little used – in part because, by way of minimising their island's carbon dioxide output, Eigg Electric's customers agreed to install limiters that keep their consumption within agreed bounds.

Three Eigg residents, or Eiggachs as islanders are known, played especially important roles in the drive to make the island grid a reality. The first is Ian Leaver, boatman, fisherman, energy consultant and, for some years, the Isle of Eigg Heritage Trust's project officer. The second is trust secretary Maggie Fyffe. The third is John Booth, a biochemist by training and an industrial relations expert by profession, who, with his wife Christine, bought a house on Eigg in 2001 and moved there from Oxfordshire in 2004.

On 1 February 2008, the Isle of Eigg entered a new era with the switching on of our island electrification project which makes 24-hour power available for the first time to all residents and businesses on the island. Until then, we were entirely dependent upon making our own power and the clattering of generators was always to be heard. Now the generators are silent, and suddenly we have leapt to the forefront of electricity generation using renewable energy resources. Our project is a world leader in the integration of multiple renewable energy sources into a grid system.

Isle of Eigg Heritage Trust website, June 2011.

In the past, a washing machine could only be used [by Eigg householders] if every other appliance was switched off … which dampened demand for energy-guzzling white goods – until now. There's been a trail of large boxes coming off the ferry in recent weeks and [Isle of Eigg Heritage] Trust secretary Maggie Fyffe is preparing to dispense with her old washboard and mangle. Every island home has been rewired to ensure 'normal' electricity flows don't blow up circuits. So now, in theory, Eiggachs could go mad and plug in everything at the same time, just like everyone else. But they won't. By mutual agreement, each house has been fitted with a limiter so the supply will trip if more than five kilowatts of electricity is used. For businesses the limit is ten kilowatts. A great example for the rest of Scotland to follow.

Lesley Riddoch, **Sunday Post,** *15 February 2008.*

It's made a huge difference to me. I used to get through a barrel of diesel a month. That cost me £150, I had all the handling involved in moving diesel barrels weighing three hundredweights each, and I had electricity for only five hours a day. Now I have 24-hour-a-day electricity at a cost of only £30 a month.

Eddie Scott, Eigg resident, speaking on BBC Scotland's **Reporting Scotland,** *28 June 2011.*

Ian's essential contribution was to raise the cash required to pay for Eigg Electric's various pieces of infrastructure – wind generators, photovoltaic arrays, dam, hydro-electric power station, cabling, storage batteries, control centre and all the rest. Maggie's vital role was to manage the funding thus obtained – juggling cash flow, ensuring compliance with grant conditions, generally keeping a tight grip on a venture of immense financial complexity. John's equally key input resulted from his agreeing, not long after he joined the heritage trust board in 2005, to become the Eigg Electrification Project's overall manager.

Eigg resident John Booth, who came to the island after community ownership had been established, played a key role in the development of the island's globally unique electricity grid – which draws on power from hydro, wind and solar sources.

'Had we gone, as was considered at the outset, for a connection to the national grid, the resulting link to the mainland would have cost at least £5 million,' Ian Leaver says. 'As it was, we had to raise just £1.6 million.' But given that Eigg's population, even after recent population growth, has still to top 100, getting 'just' £1.6 million together must surely have been a huge challenge? 'Well, it wasn't as difficult as it might have been,' Ian responds – his answer glossing over the tremendous amount of hard work he put in to secure an eventual total of £1,664,828 from (in descending order of contribution size) the European Regional Development Fund, HIE, the national lottery, the Highlands and Islands Community Energy Company, island residents, the Energy Savings Trust and Highland Council.

And what of John Booth who, on a day of wind and incessant rain, is happy to don oilskins and wellington boots prior to showing off the workings of Eigg's electricity grid to one more of the innumerable enquirers from around the world who have found their way to his home on a hillside high above the island's ferry terminal? To drive and walk in John's company from Eigg Electric's wind turbines (revolving rapidly in a near gale south-westerly), by way of the company's carefully angled slabs of photovoltaic panels (doing less well under a cloud-darkened sky), to its hydro plant (where water gushes seaward on all sides) is to be in the company of someone who is justifiably proud of what he has helped greatly to accomplish. 'I didn't know very much about electricity generation when I arrived on Eigg,' John comments. 'But when I took on the grid project management job on behalf of the trust, and on the strict condition that I kept my independence by not taking any payment for my work, I made it my business to learn.'

What John Booth learned was put to good account. There were contractors with whom he and Ian Leaver had to negotiate. There was snag after snag to be dealt with – such as the discovery that it was going to take eleven kilometres of cable, not seven as estimated, to complete Eigg Electric's transmission lines which the heritage trust was clear had to be kept underground and which, as a result, had to take unforeseen detours around hard-to-excavate pieces of terrain. There were nearly forty homes where internal wiring had to be checked, and often modernised, to make certain it was up

to scratch. There was a need to dispense with some planned items of equipment – by reducing the number of wind turbines, for example – in order to enable the heritage trust to deal with the various contingencies that arose as work went forward. 'We were trying to do something novel,' John Booth explains, 'and when you're doing something that's never been done before, you're bound to encounter difficulties.'

All difficulties were overcome, however. In Eigg Electric's operations centre, where John and Eigg Electric's four-strong team of part-time maintenance men keep a regular eye on things, the highly demanding job of meshing energy supplies from three distinct power sources – all of which perform differently in differing weather conditions – is handled with an expertise that gives the lie to the still common notion that small rural communities are incapable of running complex services. And any remaining doubts as to the significance of what Eigg Electric and the wider Isle of Eigg Heritage Trust have accomplished should have been laid to rest by the plethora of national and international awards the island has attracted. Among these, in 2010 alone, were an Ashden Award for Sustainable Energy and a £300,000 share of the £1 million prize on offer from the Big Green Challenge, a competition organised by the National Endowment for

Above, left: Eigg Electric's hydro generating plant is housed in this shed. The roofless buildings in the background testify to past depopulation in an island which, since community ownership was established, has seen population decline reversed. Right: Eigg Electric's photovoltaic cells.

Science, Technology and the Arts in order to encourage efforts to reduce the United Kingdom's carbon emissions.

The Isle of Eigg Heritage Trust is spending Big Green Challenge cash on efforts to make the island still more self-sufficient and environmentally friendly. Eigg homes are being insulated and equipped with solar water-heating panels. Car-sharing and bicycle-sharing initiatives are underway. The purchase of a community-owned electric vehicle is under consideration. Waste chip fat from the cafeterias catering for passengers on island ferries is being converted into biodiesel. Every house on the island has been provided with a compost bin. An island-based woodfuel business is up and running. 'If you don't think you can really reduce your energy consumption, then go and talk to the islanders of Eigg,' say organisers of the Ashden Awards who champion 'local energy solutions' on a worldwide basis. 'By carefully managing their energy use, actively encouraging energy-saving in everyone's daily life and generating 90 per cent of their electricity through renewable energy' this Ashden message continues, 'islanders have cut their carbon by nearly 50 per cent.'

The people whom Eigg's last private owner thought 'barmy revolutionaries', then, are today attracting not just attention but respect. Their 'example' they were told in September 2010 when Princess Anne made the first ever royal visit to their island would 'inspire others'. In the area of community ownership, it has already done so.

When people are empowered and are given intelligent support, they can make the world of difference in the fight against climate change.

Lord Puttnam, judging panel chairman, Big Green Challenge, January 2010.

Eigg's electricity grid supports four part-time maintenance jobs on the island, and residents have also been employed … to improve [Isle of Eigg Heritage] Trust properties. Likewise, the start of organised harvesting of wood for heating has created several forestry jobs for residents. A part-time 'green project manager' post has also been created, which employs two people on a job-share basis. A wider economic impact has come from having a reliable and affordable electricity supply, which has enabled several new businesses to start up … As Eigg has become known for cutting carbon emissions and protecting the environment, an increasing number of visitors have come to the island to learn about its work, bringing a further economic benefit to the residents.

The Ashden Awards for Sustainable Energy, **Case Study: Isle of Eigg Heritage Trust, May 2010.**

Yesterday there was royal endorsement for the islanders of Eigg … On the first official royal visit to the island, the Princess Royal personally thanked them for the example they had set to others across the UK. There was a time when such a tribute would have been unimaginable. But Eigg's profile has changed with its green internal grid, hailed by judges of British and international competitions as an inspiration to others … All ten of Eigg's primary school children and two-thirds of the adult population were at the village hall to welcome [Princess Anne] as she arrived in her Range Rover, specially imported for the day. A pipe tune, 'The Isle of Eigg's Welcome to the Princess Royal', had been written for the occasion by resident piper Donna MacCulloch. John Hutchison, chairman of the Isle of Eigg Heritage Trust, the community-led body that now owns the island … told the princess the community had been under the microscope of public scrutiny in recent years. 'By coming today, you … have recognised our achievements,' he said … The princess said she knew the island from sailing round it, but added: 'It is a pleasure to come ashore and see what you have achieved here … I can only say, very well done, and thank you for the example you have set because I hope that it will inspire others.'

David Ross, The Herald, *9 September 2010.*

———

On 1 May 1997 a Labour government was returned to power at Westminster. Some six weeks later, on 12 June, the Isle of Eigg Heritage Trust formally took ownership of Eigg. Among islanders' guests that day was Brian Wilson. A quarter century before, when fresh from a postgraduate course in journalism at the University of Cardiff, he had ensured that the *West Highland Free Press* adopted the land-reforming stance which made the paper the staunchest of the Eigg people's media allies in the course of their long battle with their landlords. Now both a Labour MP and a newly-appointed minister of state at the Scottish Office, where he had responsibility for Highlands and Islands matters, Brian Wilson, as he wrote subsequently, decided to make the celebrations on Eigg the occasion of a major policy announcement: 'A couple of days before the event, I phoned Iain Robertson, then chief executive of Highlands and Islands Enterprise, and told him what I was thinking of – the establishment of a Community Land Unit, within HIE, to promote and support community ownership initiatives in the Highlands and Islands.'

The establishment of HIE's Community Land Unit (CLU) was duly announced in Eigg on 12 June and, inside a week, the unit was in being. It would be headed, Iain Robertson decided, by John Watt. There could have been no better choice. Then a member of the agency's strategy team, John had joined HIE's predecessor body, the Highlands and Islands Development Board, some fifteen years earlier, and had been much involved, during the early 1980s, with the HIDB's efforts to set up and sustain community co-operatives that were, in some ways, forerunners of the land trusts that began to take shape in the 1990s. Community co-ops owned fewer assets than the later land trusts – some having been set up to manage just a single village shop. And by no means all of them survive. But community co-operatives, as their name implies, were rooted firmly in the localities they served. The experience John Watt gained when assisting their development would thus stand him in good stead in his CLU role – a role which would make him one of the key players, alongside Simon Fraser with whom John collaborated closely, in the community ownership story.

The CLU, it emerged, would be financed partly from HIE's internal resources, partly from European Union funding then available to the agency for developmental purposes. At the Scottish Office, meanwhile, Brian Wilson had secured central government cash to inject into a community land purchase fund amounting to £250,000 in the financial year 1998–99 – with a further £1 million to follow in each of the ensuing three years.

Although the CLU was to play a vital role in the subsequent expansion of community ownership, its functions and responsibilities were, to begin with, far from clear. At the outset, John Watt was expected to cope both with his existing workload and with his new duties – duties which had still to be defined. Gradually, however, his land unit role took over from his other responsibilities. At the same time, the nature of this role started to take shape. An important stage in that process was reached in the autumn of 1997 when John Watt paid a visit to Knoydart where he set about helping very directly – in a way HIE had never done before – a group of people grappling with issues reminiscent of those that had for so long confronted their counterparts on Eigg.

Despite its being part of the West Highland mainland, the Knoydart peninsula, bounded by the fiord-like inlets of Loch Hourn to the north and Loch Nevis to the south, has never been accessible by road – being served instead by ferries operating out of Mallaig. But the fact that only seventy or so people lived there in 1997 was by no means due entirely to Knoydart's inaccessibility. Once the pensinsula's population

---

Community ownership of assets is a means to supporting strong and vibrant communities. It is based on a community development approach that works *from the inside out* rather than by imposing initiatives or programmes centrally. The ownership of land and other assets is fundamental to this, providing strength and focus to communities.

SQW Consulting, **Evaluation of HIE's Community Land Unit: Final Report,** *November 2005.*

numbered around a thousand. During the early and middle decades of the nineteenth century, however, most of these people were evicted by the district's then landlords, the Macdonells of Glengarry, who had a longstanding association with the area but whose clearances – especially those that took place in the 1850s – were so comprehensive and so brutal as to become notorious even in an era accustomed to wholesale expulsions from Highlands and Islands estates. In the summer and autumn of 1853 house after house was pulled down and, when ejected families put up crude shelters made from scraps of wood and from tarpaulins, these were destroyed as well.

Towards the end of the nineteenth century, the sheep farms that took shape during the clearance period were themselves done away with and Knoydart, like lots of similar properties, became a sporting estate given over largely to the shooting, fishing and deer-stalking then indulged in increasingly by the British political and business

[In the summer of 1853] Mrs [Josephine] McDonell [of Glengarry's] factor … returned to Knoydart and commenced the work of destruction on the houses of the crofters and cottars [the latter being families without so much as a smallholding]. Not only the houses of those who had left the country [for Canada], but also the houses of those who refused to go were pulled to the ground … John McKinnon, a cottar, aged 44, is married, and has a wife and six children … When McKinnon's house was pulled down he had no place to put his head in; consequently himself and his family, for the first night or two, had to burrow among the rocks near the shore … McKinnon's wife was pregnant when she was turned out of her house … In about four days thereafter she had a premature birth; and this and [her] exposure to the elements, and the want of proper shelter and a nutritious diet, has brought on consumption, from which there is no chance whatever of her recovery.

Donald Ross, The Glengarry Evictions: Or Scenes at Knoydart, *Glasgow, 1853.*

Knoydart, although on the mainland, has no road access and is most conveniently reached by sea.

'Twas down by the farm of Scottas
Lord Brocket walked one day,
And he saw a sight that troubled him
Far more than he could say.
For the Seven Men of Knoydart
Were doing what they'd planned.
They'd staked their claim, they were
   digging drains
On Brocket's private land.

'You bloody Reds!', Lord Brocket cried,
'Wot's this you're doin' 'ere?
It doesn't pay, as you'll find today,
To insult an English peer.
For you're only Scottish half-wits,
And I'll have you understand,
You Highland swine, these hills are mine;
This is all Lord Brocket's land.'

Up spoke the men of Knoydart:
'Och, away an' shut yer trap.
For threats from a Sasunnach*
   brewer's boy,
We just don't give a rap.
For we are all ex-servicemen,
And we fought against the Hun.
We can tell our enemies by now,
And Brocket, you are one.'

* English

Hamish Henderson, 'The Seven Men of Knoydart', 1948.

establishment. The Macdonells were now long gone – their place taken by a succession of mostly absentee owners. Prominent among them was Ronald Nall-Cain or Baron Brocket, heir to a brewing fortune, who bought Knoydart in 1933. A close friend of Nazi Germany's foreign minister, Joachim von Ribbentrop, Lord Brocket was so enamoured of Adolf Hitler – to whom he had been introduced at a Nazi Party rally in Nuremberg in 1938 – that, just months before the outbreak of war in 1939, he travelled to Germany to celebrate the Führer's birthday. Their landlord's well-known Nazi sympathies gave an additional edge to a much-publicised confrontation that took place in Knoydart in 1948 when one of Brocket's farms was occupied by seven local men, some of whom were veterans of the then recent conflict with Hitler's Germany and all of whom were looking to pressurise the authorities into giving them crofts on land they believed could readily be made available for this purpose. The Seven Men of Knoydart, as the 1948 'land raiders' were dubbed by the media, failed to win their objective. However, they may have hastened Lord Brocket's subsequent disposal of his estate – which, in 1952, was once more sold.

Knoydart's 1952 purchaser was Colonel Sir Oliver Crosthwaite-Eyre. He was succeeded in 1972 by Major Nigel Chamberlayne-Macdonald who, in 1983, sold the 55,000 acre estate to Philip Rhodes, a Surrey-based property developer. No sooner had Rhodes taken charge than he proceeded to break up the property and dispose of it on a piece-by-piece basis. The final such transaction took place in 1993 when the last 18,000 acres in Philip Rhodes' possession were sold, for £1.7 million, to Reg Brealey, a north of England businessman who was chairman both of Sheffield United Football Club and a struggling jute company, Titaghur Ltd, operator of several – mostly loss-making – mills in India.

Brealey's stated aim – never realised – was to turn Knoydart into an outward-bound centre where big numbers of disadvantaged young people from Britain's cities would be provided with military-style training in an outdoor setting. This was not appealing to Knoydart's few remaining residents who lived for the most part in the little village of Inverie where ferries call regularly in summer and a bit less regularly in winter. What was still less appealing – indeed downright disconcerting – was the manner in which these people, for much of the 1990s, found it almost impossible to be sure who their landlord was. At one point, the Knoydart Estate was thought to belong to Reg Brealey personally; at another it was said to be owned by Titaghur; next it had been transferred to a company named Knoydart Pensinsula Ltd (KPL) which itself underwent various ownership changes that ended, as Knoydart people learned in early 1998, in its being controlled by a further businessman, Stephen Hinchcliffe, whose Facia trading empire – owner of high street stores like Saxone and Sock Shop – had collapsed two years previously with debts in excess of £100 million. Hinchcliffe, whose role in the Facia debacle was soon to be under investigation both by the Serious Fraud Office and the Department of Trade and Industry, was eventually jailed for five years on corruption charges. In these circumstances, it was perfectly predictable that Knoydart Peninsula Ltd's Inverie-based employees, like their counterparts on Maruma's Eigg, should have ceased to receive any wages. Nor was it surprising that Knoydart people were increasingly of a mind that, if their locality was to have any sort of worthwhile future, they needed first to be rid forever of ownership of the KPL variety.

By 1997 – when HIE's Community Land Unit, in the person of John Watt, began to take an active interest in Knoydart – the Knoydart Community Association, representing local residents, had combined with a number of other groups to create an organisation capable, when the opportunity arose, of mounting a bid for KPL's landholdings. This organisation was the Knoydart Foundation. An approximate equivalent of the Isle of Eigg Heritage Trust, the foundation allied the community association with Highland Council, the John Muir Trust, the Chris Brasher Trust and Kilchoan Estate. The John Muir Trust (JMT), a wild land conservation charity named after a Scots-born environmentalist who pioneered national parks in the United States, already had a stake in Knoydart where it had bought – from Philip Rhodes – a 3,100 acre property on the peninsula's north coast. The Chris Brasher Trust, established by the athlete, journalist and London marathon co-founder of the same name, was closely associated with JMT – which Brasher had helped set up. The owners of the Kilchoan Estate wished simply to bring an end to the problems plaguing a property next door to their own. And Highland Council had become involved for reasons identical to those that had led to its close engagement with Eigg.

The present Knoydart Estate [consists of] … the remains of a far greater estate totalling 55,000 acres which, following acquisition by a private owner [Philip Rhodes] in 1983, was fragmented through selling off houses and parcels of land of varying size … The estate suffers severely from twenty years of asset-stripping, with a total lack of maintenance or modernisation in recent years.

Graeme Scott and Steve Westbrook, Knoydart Foundation: Business and Development Plan, March 2000.

In November 1997 the Knoydart Foundation, following Assynt and Eigg precedent, launched an appeal for the cash that would be needed to realise its ownership ambitions – the foundation's appeal leaflets being financed, thanks to John Watt's intervention and in HIE's first gesture of this kind, by the CLU. Raising the requisite amount of money proved difficult – the foundation not being helped by the national lottery's Heritage Memorial Fund refusing, as it had done already in the case of Eigg, to give any assistance. By no means all the necessary cash had been got together when, more than a year later, the Knoydart Foundation began to negotiate a possible purchase deal with the Bank of Scotland – KPL's principal creditor and, as such, anxious to salvage loans secured against the Knoydart Estate. 'We had to find £750,000 in total,' recalls Charlie King who lives in Mallaig and who, as the councillor representing Knoydart on Highland Council, also represented the local authority on the Knoydart Foundation. The foundation's public appeal had raised some £150,000. Substantial sums were also on the table from the John Muir Trust, the Chris Brasher Trust, HIE, Scottish Natural Heritage (the government's conservation agency) and Cameron Mackintosh, a London-based theatre impresario who had bought an estate near Mallaig some years previously. 'But we were still short of what was needed,' Charlie King says. 'Then Chris Brasher persuaded one of his friends to make an anonymous donation of £100,000 and, from the Bank of Scotland's head office on the Mound in Edinburgh, where we were trying to clinch a deal, I got on the phone to HIE and managed to get the CLU's original offer of £40,000 upped by another £35,000 – which meant that Cameron Mackintosh, who'd promised to match the CLU's contribution, increased his donation as well. It had been touch and go. But we were there.'

On 26 March 1999, the day the Knoydart Foundation formally gained control of the Knoydart Estate, local farmer Iain Wilson remarked that Knoydart residents and their foundation partners had a responsibility to ensure that the next generation of Knoydart people inherited an estate in better shape than it was when the foundation took over. This challenge has been met. 'Knoydart today is doing well,' Charlie King comments. 'I'm proud to have been associated with the 1999 buy-out and with all that's since been achieved by people who'd never have had the chance to prosper if Knoydart had remained in the hands of absentee landlords.'

This is a day I thought would never come to fruition. There have been so many ups and downs and twists and turns. But we have made it, and I am absolutely delighted. We have a community buy-out, and we can now begin the hard work of community management.

Councillor Charlie King, March 1999: **West Highland Free Press, 5 March 1999.**

Many people talk about partnerships, but here in Knoydart we are at the sharp end in delivering a partnership which is very much in tune with the times and which offers the very best hope for one of the most wild and beautiful places in the country – and for its local community.

Nigel Hawkins, director, John Muir Trust, March 1999: **West Highland Free Press, 5 March 1999.**

The definition of custody, as I understand it, means guardianship or protective care. We don't really own the land – nobody does. We are only stewards of it for as long as we are here. We, as a community, accept the challenge to take care of it and to try to pass it on to the next generation in a slightly better state than that in which we received it.

Iain Wilson, hill farmer, Knoydart, April 1999: **West Highland Free Press, 2 April 1999.**

The Knoydart Foundation is a company limited by guarantee with charitable status … The Foundation aims to manage the Knoydart Estate as an area of employment and settlement on the Knoydart Peninsula without detriment to its natural beauty and character and to seek and encourage the preservation of its landscape, wildlife, natural resources, culture and rural heritage.

Knoydart Foundation website, July 2011.

What particularly pleases him, Charlie says, is that Knoydart today contains many more young folk than it did ten or fifteen years ago. Two of them are sisters Isla and Rhona Miller who grew up in Knoydart and who, following a stint in Glasgow where they studied pottery and ceramics, came home to start their own business, Knoydart Pottery and Tearoom, located in one of the several buildings acquired by the Knoydart Foundation back in 1999. 'This is a great place to live,' Isla insists. 'There's always something going on. There's a great sense of community. Yes, we have to make our own entertainment. But with more and more people around, we're getting pretty good at that.'

Isla and Rhona's Inverie tearoom – where the bacon rolls, this customer can testify, are of the highest quality – stands right beside the sea in the middle of Inverie. Across the road – a road, remember, that is internal to Knoydart and does not go anywhere else – is the Knoydart Foundation's office. The person in charge there is Angela Williams, the foundation's development manager who was appointed to this post – part-financed initially by HIE's Community Land Unit – in 2001. Before coming to Knoydart, which she had never visited until she stepped off the ferry for her interview with Knoydart Foundation representatives, Angela was employed by an environmental regeneration organisation in Lancashire. Now she and her husband, together with their

High above the mountains
the golden eagles soar.
Our spirits rise to meet them,
we're shackle-bound no more.
We look now to the future and
to make our promise true:
To keep Knoydart wild and wonderful,
a home for me and you.

Pupils of Knoydart Primary School, March 1999.

two children, are firmly established in Knoydart which – in the time Angela has been here and thanks in no small part to her efforts – has changed greatly for the better.'

Like Eigg, Knoydart has never been connected to the national grid. Unlike Eigg, the Knoydart Estate had been provided by one of its previous owners, Nigel Chamberlayne-Macdonald, with a hydro-electricity supply. But as was true of everything else on the estate, neither Knoydart's small power station nor its associated equipment had received much in the way of attention or maintenance during the twenty years previous to 1999. It was consequently a Knoydart Foundation priority to refurbish these facilities. Because Knoydart, like Eigg, was in the part of the Highland Council area for which John Hutchison was responsible, he had been appointed the foundation's company secretary. And because John was a civil engineer by training, he played a leading part in planning and organising the work needed to get Knoydart's hydro infrastructure into reasonable shape – this work being financed in part by Highland Council and by HIE.

Left: *Angela Williams of the Knoydart Foundation at the foundation's office.* **Right:** *Rhona Miller in the Knoydart tearoom and pottery which she runs with her sister, Isla.*

The Knoydart Foundation inherited a portfolio of assets in poor condition – and inherently unprofitable ... [These] assets [now] generate sufficient revenue [to allow the foundation] to at least break even annually. The Knoydart Estate now has a substantially improved infrastructure and services compared to its condition on acquisition by the community in 1999 ... The relative stability that Knoydart Foundation ownership provides for the local population appears to have encouraged community confidence and capacity. This is reflected in business growth ... by established businesses ... and by newer operations ... It is also demonstrated by [the] number of young people who have returned, post-education, to live and work in the area.

Campbell Consulting, **An Independent Review of the Knoydart Foundation,** *June 2008.*

When people hear that we run our own hydro electric scheme for the community, it's not uncommon for them to ask whether everyone gets free electricity. If only! Everyone who connects to the system pays a unit rate of 12p. This income is used to pay for wages, maintenance, insurance and other running costs. Any surplus to date has been invested in upgrading the rest of the distribution system.

Knoydart Foundation website, July 2011.

Left: *The Knoydart Foundation's ranger, Tommy McManmon, welcomes some of Knoydart's many visitors.* Right: *A walking party leaving Knoydart for Mallaig.*

As Angela Williams stresses, more requires to be done to make Knoydart's power supply totally reliable. But its already being a lot more reliable than previously is one factor in the recent expansion of Knoydart's economy – enterprises like Rhona and Isla Miller's pottery and tearoom depending, for obvious reasons, on the availability of electricity.

Economic growth has been accompanied, and boosted further, by a marked surge in population – which, at around 120, has grown by more than 60 per cent since 1999. As levels of business activity have increased, as facilities for tourists (whose numbers are constantly increasing) have been upgraded, as estate-owned homes have been modernised and new homes built, rents and other revenues due to the Knoydart Estate have risen substantially. Although the grant aid once received from the CLU to

A couple of Knoydart's younger residents, Heather Gilmour and Anna Wilson (left) who works in the Knoydart Foundation's always busy bunkhouse.

help with administrative costs has long since ceased, estate books are consequently in balance – something that was seldom, if ever, pulled off when Knoydart was owned by private landlords. 'Achieving financial sustainability was one of our basic aims,' Angela Williams comments. 'Given all the outgoings we have on wages, maintenance and much else, it's not been easy to get there. But we've managed it – and this matters. After all, community ownership can only work long-term if a community-owned estate can be made to break even or, better still, can be got into profit.'

———————

As it became evident in the mid-1990s that the Labour Party was likely to win the general election that was bound to be held in either 1996 or 1997, and as it became equally clear that Labour, if returned to government, would devolve power to a Scottish parliament, there began to be debate – just as there had been in the 1970s when devolution was last on the agenda – about what such a parliament might do by way of promoting land reform. This debate was given focus when Robin Callander, a Deeside-based policy consultant with a close interest in land-related topics got together a number of kindred spirits and set about organising a series of public lectures in memory of John McEwen who had died in 1992 – just two days short of his 105th birthday. I contributed to this series in September 1995 when I suggested, first, that a Scottish parliament which shied away from land reform would be a parliament not worth having and, second, that Labour, in order to ensure that a future Scottish parliament was well placed to legislate on land, should start work on a Land Reform Bill in advance of such a parliament actually taking shape.

My opinions were neither here nor there. The opinions of Donald Dewar, who became Secretary of State for Scotland following Labour's landslide victory in the eventual election of 1 May 1997, mattered a great deal. The manifesto on which he and his colleagues came to power had included a promise 'to initiate a study into the system of land ownership and management in Scotland'. Although fulfilment of this pledge was put on hold until Dewar knew for sure there would be a Scottish parliament, the September 1997 referendum which gave overwhelming backing to devolution was followed in October by the Scottish Secretary's establishment of a Land

A parliament which is prepared to act decisively on land will be a parliament which will thus demonstrate its willingness to alter Scotland fundamentally. A parliament which, conversely, shies away from land reform will be a parliament which, by its dodging of this most symbolic issue, will make clear that, though we shall again have our own legislature, great consequences will not follow from that fact.

James Hunter, **Towards a Land Reform Agenda for a Scots Parliament: The Second John McEwen Memorial Lecture,** *September 1995.*

Land is a key resource. The life chances of people living in rural areas depend on how it is used. All too often in the past, the interests of the majority have been damaged by the interests of the few who control that resource.

Land Reform Policy Group, Identifying the Problems, *February 1998.*

Community ownership is clearly not appropriate in all situations, but it is an option to be considered … Involvement of local people in the management of land can increase the local skills base and lead to increased community confidence, stronger community identity and population retention.

Land Reform Policy Group, Identifying the Problems, *February 1998.*

Reform Policy Group whose task was 'to identify and assess proposals for land reform in rural Scotland'.

Some members of Donald Dewar's ministerial team at the Scottish Office were anxious to make certain that these proposals were drawn up in advance of their becoming the responsibility of a devolved administration which, these ministers felt, might not be as convinced as they were of the need for radical initiatives. Brian Wilson was very much of this view. While not directly involved in the work of the Land Reform Policy group, he had an ally in John Sewel who, being responsible for agriculture and the environment, took personal charge of the group – thus ensuring that its work was completed (more speedily than might otherwise have been the case) in the course of 1998. The policy group's recommendations, Donald Dewar stressed in the course of his own contribution to the McEwen Memorial Lecture series, would be picked up by a soon-to-be-elected Scottish administration – if, of course, that administration (as proved to be the case) included Labour. 'There is undoubtedly a powerful symbolism, which attracts me greatly, in land reform being amongst the first actions of our new Scottish parliament,' Donald Dewar told his McEwen Lecture audience in Aviemore in September 1998. Presiding over the launch of the Land Reform Policy Group's 'Recommendations for Action' the following January, the Secretary of State was still more forthright: 'Land reform, for so long an issue out of the spotlight, has now moved firmly centre stage. There is a consensus across Scotland that legislation to break down barriers to land reform should be one of the first acts of the Scottish parliament.' Such legislation, the Land Reform Policy Group urged strongly, should include measures intended to make community ownership much easier to achieve.

We are committed to assisting communities in Scotland who wish to assume greater responsibility for their own future through the acquisition and management of the land on which they live. The promotion of community involvement in land – including the option of land ownership – is entirely in line with the government's commitment to land reform.

Donald Dewar, Secretary of State for Scotland, December 1998: West Highland Free Press, 4 December 1998.

In the course of the 1990s, then, community ownership, which – despite the Stornoway Trust example – previously featured nowhere on policy agendas, became not just an attainable reality but one which governments and their agencies began increasingly to advocate and aid. This process had begun – a little falteringly – with Russell Sanderson's abortive attempt to persuade crofters in Skye and Raasay to take over the management of government-owned land. It had been given new impetus and new direction when communities in Assynt, Eigg and elsewhere managed to buy land that had formerly been in private ownership. And from 1997 onwards, with the establishment of HIE's Community Land Unit and the setting up of the Land Reform Policy Group, the time was ripe for new experiments in the ownership and management of land. This made it possible, in October 1997, for Skye and Lochalsh Enterprise (SALE), the HIE subsidiary responsible for economic development in that part of the Highlands and Islands, to persuade its parent body to buy the 4,500 acre Orbost Estate.*

Orbost, in the same north-western corner of Skye as Glendale, with which the estate shares a boundary, had been comprehensively cleared in the nineteenth century. By the 1990s, though still containing the ruins of lots of long-since-emptied dwellings, the place was home to only a small number of people. SALE aimed to boost that number – and to do so in a manner that would make some contribution to meeting the soaring local demand for both houses and crofts.

This demand resulted from the fact that, for some years, many more people had been moving on to the island than were leaving. Nobody had predicted that development. Between the 1840s and the 1960s, Skye's total population had fallen inexorably – from around 24,000 to not much more than 6,000. Much of the rest of the Highlands and Islands had experienced similar population losses. And for all that the Highlands and Islands Development Board had been set up in the mid-1960s with the stated objective of reversing those trends, there had been little expectation of

---

*   One more declaration of interest. From 1995 to 1998, I chaired Skye and Lochalsh Enterprise and, in this capacity, was committed strongly to SALE's Orbost initiative.

The blueprint for land reform, published this week by the Secretary of State for Scotland [Donald Dewar], has matched our hopes and exceeded our expectations. Let there be no mistake. If these proposals are translated into legislation, the pattern of landownership, and the balance of social relationships which accompany it will be transformed for ever. This is a landmark occasion which the *West Highland Free Press* has lived and worked for.

West Highland Free Press *editorial, 8 January 1999.*

The approach to Orbost.

Skye and Lochalsh has experienced substantial population growth in the last 25 years, probably the fastest in Scotland. This has put pressure on the provision of housing … and [on] access to crofting land. Dunvegan and the area bordering the Orbost Estate is part of this growth pattern, with a diversifying local economy … Current pressure on housing stock is forecast to increase … There are currently 54 family units on the area's housing list … The Orbost Estate, a hill farm comprising 4,300 acres of rough grazing and 200 acres of inbye [meaning cultivable land] came on the market unexpectedly in September 1997. There was some concern locally that the land could be purchased by outside interests and that employment opportunities would be lost. Following an appraisal of the potential of the estate and two well-attended public meetings which gave support for the initiative, the land was purchased by HIE in October 1997.

Highlands and Islands Enterprise, Board Paper, April 1998.

this actually happening. But it did. Between 1970 and the twentieth century's end, a period when the population of Scotland as a whole was more or less static, Highlands and Islands population rose by something like a fifth – with the Skye total rising by nearly 20 per cent in the 1980s alone.* Many of the island's incomers, moreover, were young folk – in their twenties and thirties. This was good news from a developmental perspective – people in that age group being generally the most active economically. It was less good news for anyone – newcomer or established resident – trying to find a place to stay. As population pressure increased, the price of houses rose steeply. So did the cost of taking over a croft – crofts being in particular demand because a significant proportion of Skye's in-migrants were intent on combining their other occupations with the management of a piece of land.

Orbost in 1997 already contained some owner-occupied homes. The estate, however, had been operated essentially as a hill farm by the family from whom SALE bought the property for about £500,000. The agency's intention, then, was to grow the existing community substantially by making some house-sites available for purchase (ideally at low prices) and by creating new homes for rent alongside a number of croft-type smallholdings, workshops and other business premises of that kind. Once this new community was up and running, it was envisaged, the people who were part of it might want – might indeed be encouraged – to take Orbost into community ownership.

SALE's Orbost initiative was in some ways an attempt to do again what had been done on a much larger scale in the years between 1900 and 1930, both in Skye and other parts of the Highlands and Islands, by the Congested District Board and the

---

* This is not the place to explore what it is that has attracted so many people to the Highlands and Islands in recent decades. Among key factors, however, are the region's highly attractive natural environment, its quality of life and the fact that, thanks to the information technologies now available, distance from markets is no longer the barrier to economic activity that it once was. In Skye's case, new jobs were also becoming available in tourism, at the island's Gaelic college, in fish farms, electronics and other new enterprises.

Board of Agriculture for Scotland – organisations which, as noted earlier, had created hundreds of new crofts on land (some of it close to Orbost) bought for this purpose. But what had been accomplished with comparative ease by agencies operating with little or no public consultation proved more challenging for one committed, as SALE was, to keeping people informed of its intentions. At well-attended public meetings in Dunvegan in October 1997, SALE – which would not otherwise have proceeded with its purchase plans – obtained a great deal of backing for its proposals. But a lot of this backing was lost in the months that followed. There was no local consensus, it emerged, as to what exactly should happen at Orbost – with people favouring outcomes as divergent as the retention of the former farming operation and the conversion of much of the estate's arable land into a golf course. There was criticism of the type of settlement – with housing clustered together rather than dispersed as in typical crofting townships – which SALE was suggesting. There was censure of the way in which it was proposed to allocate homes and holdings. Above all, there was growing feeling to the effect that both SALE and HIE were not taking on board what was being said locally. This arose in part from the fact that both agencies, because of their being involved in something that was new to them, were less than clear about their ultimate objectives and, as a result, took longer than they should have done to decide exactly what they were about. In these circumstances, it came as no great surprise that the various community groups represented on an Orbost advisory committee eventually withdrew their representatives – leaving SALE and HIE to try as best they could to accommodate the wishes of those people who, despite everything, wanted very much to move on to the estate.

Among this group were Keith and Rachael Jackson, then in their twenties. Keith had been eleven when his parents moved to Skye from Northumberland. Rachael, an Australian who grew up in New South Wales and studied animal science at university in Sydney, first came to Skye as a student – attracted by the fact that her paternal grandmother's emigrant grandfather belonged to a family resident for centuries on the island. Returning to Skye in 1997 after completing her studies, Rachael Staas, as she then was, met Keith Jackson, then a shepherd in the Dunvegan area. 'We married in 1998,' Rachael says. 'Both Keith and I wanted to make our home in Skye, but

Rachael Jackson and her children, Jess and Tristan, at Orbost Farm.

we couldn't find anywhere to live. Highlands and Islands Enterprise had just bought Orbost, and we applied for a place here. At that point, however, we were turned down – so we had to go off to Perthshire where Keith got a shepherd's post that came with a house. We spent three years in Perthshire, but it wasn't at all like Skye. I never felt at home there. Keith wasn't happy either, and we were thinking about leaving Scotland when we saw that HIE were advertising a new set of holdings at Orbost. This time we were lucky.'

During 2010, HIE decided to offer – on a competitive basis – the 4,000 or so acres of hill grazings constituting Orbost Farm to prospective tenants. There was substantial interest in the tenancy which the Jacksons were keen to get and which, to their obvious delight, they succeeded in obtaining. Today, then, Keith, Rachael and their two children, Tristan and Jess, have graduated, as Rachael puts it, from the smallholding they previously operated and are, as a result, expanding the agricultural and other enterprises they have developed since getting back to Skye.

On a morning of intermittent rain, and in a farmhouse kitchen filled with the enticing aroma of new-baked cakes, Keith Jackson talks about his and Rachael's plans. These involve many miles of new fencing, an expansion of the couple's cattle herd from fifty to 100 animals, a still greater expansion of the their sheep flock, the retention of their pigs and hens – and, perhaps, the acquisition of some goats (goat meat, as Keith points out, being much in demand in today's Britain). Nor are the Jacksons content simply to rear animals for sale. They are already much involved in retailing meat and meat products from Orbost – and are intent on doing a lot more of this.

There are several other young families besides the Jacksons in today's Orbost where there are more children than at any time in very many years. Half a dozen smallholdings and several new homes – some rented and some in private ownership – have taken shape. Workshops have gone up, businesses have been established, woodland is being expanded – and footpath provision has made it easier for visitors to access what remains a beautiful part of Skye.

For the last nine years, Keith and I have been building ... a business ... based on the principles of slow food production – the aim is to produce the best quality, fantastic-tasting meat products from slowly-reared, traditional breed animals. It's simple food, and food with provenance. And we are privileged enough to be able to work the land, care for the animals, and produce this food in one of the more beautiful settings in the world – Orbost on the Isle of Skye in Scotland. In March 2009 we appeared in a BBC [television] series called 'Monty Hall's Great Escape'. It was a great project to be involved with, where we could share our years of hard-learnt knowledge with Monty while he escaped from the bright lights of the city to live on the west coast of Scotland for six months and to try his hand at the crofting life. Monty took charge of some of our Soay Sheep and two of our beautiful Iron Age Pigs, and we were there along the way to help him out and advise him. It's now 2011, and Keith and I ... are in a 15-year tenancy of Orbost Farm [where we] plan to increase our herds and expand production. It's a very exciting, but somewhat daunting, undertaking. We're up for the challenge though, and hope to create a sustainable, successful and balanced farming unit here at Orbost.

Keith and Rachael Jackson's Blog, July 2011.

'We have a good community here,' Rachael Jackson comments. But she is sensitive to what has gone before and to difficulties that – inevitably – attracted considerable publicity. 'There were people living here before the HIE purchase,' Rachael says. 'Then others of us arrived in what must have seemed an artificial sort of way. We're all neighbours now. But even though Keith and I have benefited enormously from what happened, I can understand why HIE and Skye and Lochalsh Enterprise found themselves in so much trouble.'

Paradoxically, the process of achieving a degree of unity among Orbost's newer and more established households has been helped by the Jacksons and other comparatively recent arrivals having had their own issues with Highlands and Islands Enterprise – which (SALE and similar HIE offshoots having been wound up in 2007) is now in

Alex Kozikowski, a woodworker who acquired his home at Orbost as a result of Highlands and Islands Enterprise having bought the estate.

sole charge of the Orbost Estate. From Rachael's perspective, HIE first pressed Orbost residents to opt for community ownership – and then told them that such ownership was no longer possible. 'All of us put so much effort into the planning asked of us in the run-up to what we thought would be an eventual hand-over of the estate to its residents,' Rachael Jackson explains. 'We're all busy people. We're mostly bringing up small children, mostly developing our own businesses. But we found the time to map out how community ownership might take shape here. We worked really, really hard on this. Then the plug was pulled on us. That was pretty devastating.'

The origins of HIE's apparent retreat from community ownership at Orbost are bound up with wider policy issues to which this book returns in conclusion. Back in 1997, a year that had begun with Michael Forsyth insisting that land in public ownership could be transferred to its occupants for nothing, SALE had assumed that

Land in intensive cultivation at Orbost.

Orbost would one day be made over to its residents at minimal cost to them. Ten or so years later, with these residents anxious to take ownership of the property – and engaged actively in the planning Rachael Jackson describes – ministers and civil servants in Edinburgh were adamant that such a thing could not be done. HIE attempts to find some way of getting Orbost into community ownership at an affordable cost foundered on repeated rulings that public assets could only be disposed of at market price. This same stance, as mentioned previously, badly delayed West Harris's transfer to its residents. In the Orbost case, the estate being theoretically worth several hundred thousand pounds, the abandonment of the Forsyth line of 1997 has made community acquisition unattainable – the only other likely source of help with such an acquisition having been closed off by the national lottery (which had a key role, as will be seen, in several post-2000 community purchases) being unwilling (for reasons set out later) to finance the transfer to communities of properties already in public ownership.

As this book's last chapter will underline, it is hard to understand why politicians thus make so much of market value in relation to the disposal of land in the possession of public agencies – whether HIE, the Scottish government's own agricultural department or the Forestry Commission. Where community ownership has been established, after all, it has proved a first-rate way of securing a wide range of nationally-agreed objectives – having to do with population retention, housing provision, economic growth and much else. What has taken place in Eigg and Knoydart proves this. What has happened in Gigha proves it too.

The southern approach to the North Harris Estate.

5

AT LAST WE COULD FORCE THE PACE

Isle of Gigha Heritage Trust
Abriachan Forest Trust
Land Reform Act
North Harris Trust
Bhaltos Community Trust
Urras Oighreachd Ghabhsainn
Stòras Uibhist

Dairy cattle on Gigha.

CHAPTER FIVE

At last we could force the pace

Isle of Gigha Heritage Trust § Abriachan Forest Trust
Land Reform Act § North Harris Trust § Bhaltos Community Trust
Urras Oighreachd Ghabhsainn § Stòras Uibhist

The morning of Friday 15 March 2002 was cold and damp in Gigha, with a gusty wind out of the south-east shoving squalls of icy rain across the island. So strong was the wind, in fact, that it looked for a time as if the Gigha ferry might not be able to make its regular crossings from Tayinloan on the Argyll mainland. This was a worry – because the ferry that morning was expected to be unusually busy. Lots of people of Gigha extraction – people who had gone to live elsewhere in the course of the preceding twenty or thirty years – were on their way home. Also bound for Gigha that same morning were representatives of various public agencies – plus several local and national politicians. Among the latter was a member (Wendy Alexander) of the first Scottish government to have taken office in nearly 300 years – as well as a member (Brian Wilson) of the other government (Britain's) with a continuing interest in Scotland. All those folk – weather, as always in the Hebrides, permitting – were intent on being on Gigha by midday to witness, and participate in, a ceremony which all of them expected (correctly as events have proved) to constitute a turning point in the island's history.

That history was similar to Eigg's. Both islands, though separated by many miles of ocean, had been part of the medieval Lordship of the Isles. Then, following the lordship's late-fifteenth-century collapse, each had been controlled by clan chiefs or lairds of more or less local background until, a little later in Gigha's case than Eigg's, the two islands began to be bought, sold and bought again by monied men from far away. Of these, Gigha people say, the best – from their perspective – was Sir James Horlick whose family had prospered on the back of the malted drink that bears their name. Horlick acquired Gigha in 1944 and, like his Runciman contemporaries in Eigg, spent heavily on the property. But as is evident from the experience of estate after estate all over the Highlands and Islands, ownership of this type, however helpful in the short run, is inherently unstable – even the most benevolent landlords, assuming that they themselves do not run out of cash or develop other enthusiasms, being rarely provided with equally benevolent heirs. So it was with James Horlick. On his death in 1972, Gigha was promptly sold – the island then changing hands no fewer than three times in just twenty years.

One Gigha laird, Malcolm Potier, a property developer, lasted not much more than thirty months. First Potier was bankrupted – something that led to his island tenants finding eviction notices pinned to their front doors when one of their landlord's creditors tried to obtain vacant possession of his Gigha properties. Next Potier received successive and lengthy jail sentences in Australia where Gigha's ex-owner, as he was by this stage, twice attempted to hire a hitman to kill his former lover whose daughter Potier had earlier abducted.

Potier, described regularly (if a little inadequately) in the British media as 'colourful', was reported at the time of his purchase of Gigha in 1989 to have outbid rock star Mick Jagger. He had fallen in love with the island after spending a holiday there, Potier told one journalist. 'For years,' he said, 'I dreamed of owning the place much as a child yearns for a train set.'

Perhaps nothing is more illustrative of what is wrong with the sort of land ownership that has for so long been common in the Highlands and Islands than the fact that whole localities can thus be regarded – literally – as playthings. Nor did Potier's departure for the Australian prison system bring much in the way of badly-needed stability to Gigha. Purchased by another businessman in 1992, the island, after just nine years, was again put up for sale.

Gigha's resident community, by this point, seemed set on the road to extinction. The island's population, once above 400, had dipped below the hundred mark. Not all the reasons for this decline stemmed from the nature of Gigha's ownership, but many did. Firmly in this category was the quite appalling state of the bulk of island

If you want people to stay on [an] island, you have to have houses they are happy to live in, and some of ours were described as the worst he had ever seen by … [a] housing surveyor.

Kenny Robison, Gigha farmer, speaking to the managing committee of the Scottish Land Fund, May 2002.

One of the major factors in [Gigha's] population decline has been the lack of good-quality, warm, dry, affordable housing … In the 34 years prior to community purchase there was [just] one house built on Gigha and for many decades there has been no significant investment in the housing stock.

Isle of Gigha Housing Improvement Project, Project Brief, July 2003.

homes – Gigha being one of those properties where not just the land but almost the entire housing stock belonged to the place's mostly absentee owners. While there had been investment in this stock during the Horlick era, subsequent lairds – some of them lacking capital, others lacking inclination and all of them, because ownership changed so often, lacking time – had not sanctioned any substantial expenditure either on housing or other facilities. At the start of the twenty-first century, it followed, housing conditions on Gigha were among the worst in the United Kingdom. When surveyed professionally in 2002, three-quarters of the forty or so estate-owned homes on the island were found to be below the officially tolerable standard. Of the remainder, all – bar a single dwelling – were described as being 'in serious disrepair'. A Gigha resident, it was calculated, was eighty times more likely to be living in a substandard dwelling than were people in Scotland as a whole.

Nothing of this featured in sale particulars issued at the start of August 2001. There Gigha was described as 'one of the finest Scottish islands in private ownership' – the property's attractions including its being only 'thirty minutes by helicopter' from Glasgow Airport. A community purchase, evidently, was not envisaged by the selling agents. Nor was it contemplated, to begin with, by more than a small minority of islanders. When George Lyon, who represented Argyll and Bute in the recently established Scottish parliament, called a public meeting on Gigha in mid-August and suggested that a community buy-out might be worth considering, he found only fourteen backers. Many more Gigha people were either hostile to such a buy-out or thought community ownership could not be made to work. This is understandable. For a long time, families had been quitting this island where living conditions were shockingly poor, where economic activity was minimal and where opportunity was next best to non-existent. There was no chance, in these circumstances, of their Liberal Democrat MSP's initiative being greeted with acclaim by Gigha residents. In shrinking and demoralised communities, risk-taking is hard to contemplate. It is natural in such communities for pessimism to be more prevalent than its opposite.

But for all their initial scepticism, Gigha people were persuaded to agree with George Lyon that it would do no harm to hear more about what community ownership might entail. Towards the end of August, John Watt, still in charge of HIE's Community Land Unit, duly arrived on Gigha in the company of Simon Fraser, the Stornoway solicitor whose involvement with the community ownership movement – in Assynt, Eigg and elsewhere – was, by this point, more than ten years old. As well as speaking with islanders collectively, Fraser and Watt met privately with those individuals and families who wanted additional detail. This helped set anxieties to rest and, at a further public meeting towards the end of August, Gigha residents decided to set up a six-person steering group with a remit to explore matters further. This group was chaired by Willie McSporran whose family roots went deep in Gigha and who, prior to his taking on this new and demanding role, had thought himself at the end of a long and varied career involving stints as a farm worker, fisherman, estate handyman and ferryman.

With the help of funding made available by the CLU, Willie McSporran and his colleagues commissioned work on a study of what it would take both to get Gigha into community ownership and to ensure that such ownership delivered worthwhile benefits. Among the authors of this study was Oban-based accountant Lorne MacLeod. 'Because Gigha is a long way from places like Assynt, Eigg or Knoydart, and because it's very definitely outside the circulation area of the *West Highland Free Press*,' Lorne MacLeod says, 'people there hadn't been exposed to all the debates and arguments about community ownership which had been going on for several years further north. That's why it was so important that the steering group were given the chance, courtesy of the CLU, to send a delegation to Eigg where community ownership, by the summer of 2001, had been an established fact for more than four years.'

On Eigg towards the end of September, the Gigha steering group's representatives met with, and were shown around by, Maggie Fyffe and her Isle of Eigg Heritage Trust colleagues. 'This visit was pivotal to our thinking,' farmer Kenny Robison, one of the Gigha residents who travelled to Eigg, said subsequently. 'What really impressed us was that people on Eigg had great pride in what they were doing. There was a very good feeling about the community. Just as important, our visit showed us what could happen [Eigg still bearing the marks of the extreme neglect it had experienced] if we left ourselves open to having a really bad landlord.' But if Kenny Robison, Willie

Willie McSporran, the Isle of Gigha Heritage Trust's first chairman and a key figure in the community ownership movement.

McSporran and fellow steering group members were starting to be convinced of the merits of following Eigg people's example, nobody knew for certain at the end of September – with the closing date for offers only four weeks away – if other islanders were of the same mind. In order to find out, a postal ballot was organised with the help of Argyll and Bute Council, the local authority which administers Gigha. On 5 October, voting papers were sent to all 89 people on the island's electoral roll. Of the 89 papers issued, 82 were returned and, of these, 58 – some 71 per cent of the total – endorsed a community buy-out attempt of exactly the sort that had met with such a lukewarm response when George Lyon first floated this idea.

When explaining what had changed in the interim, Kenny Robison stressed that, to begin with, Gigha people lacked confidence in their own collective capacities. 'We had lost the feeling that we could control anything,' he commented. 'Our population was declining. In twenty years, we had dropped from 180 to 98. Our tenanted farms were being abandoned. When I came to the island as a farmer twenty years ago there were ten working farms and now there are only three. There were twenty-eight children in the primary school and now there are only six.' Gigha residents had begun by thinking there was nothing they could do to reverse those trends, Kenny Robison went on. But in the light of the information that had come their way since the island's sale was announced, they had come round to the view that a community ownership bid might be their last best chance to put right what had gone so very badly wrong. 'We had reached a point in our history,' Kenny Robison said, 'when we were faced with collapsing completely as a community or taking our destiny into our own hands.'

This was all very well. But the asking price for Gigha was £3.85 million – two and a half times what had been paid for Eigg. How were fewer than a hundred people to find such a sum? That difficulty (which, given the speed at which the requisite amount had to be raised, would otherwise have been insurmountable) was got over with the help of the Scottish Land Fund (SLF).

A ring-fenced subset of the much bigger New Opportunities Fund which was responsible for spending a substantial slice of the cash generated by the national lottery,

It's all about having confidence to take control of one's future. We don't have any regrets, and we will be encouraging the delegation from Gigha to follow our lead.

Maggie Fyffe, Isle of Eigg Heritage Trust, September 2001: Scotsman, 27 September 2001.

the SLF had been established by the UK's Labour government as a result, in large part, of internal lobbying by one of its ministers, Brian Wilson, now with the Department of Energy but still keeping in close touch with Highlands and Islands matters. Having advocated the creation of a lottery-financed 'National Land Fund' as far back as 1996, and having helped ensure that a recommendation to this effect was included in the Land Reform Policy Group's final report, Brian Wilson was much involved in the SLF's establishment – and in the appointment, as the fund's chairman, of David Campbell, an Ayrshire businessman who also chaired the New Opportunities Fund's Scottish committee and who, in his land fund role, was to prove an enthusiastic and committed supporter of the community ownership concept.

Seen from the outset as a means of ensuring that new community initiatives were not shut out from lottery funding in the way that the Isle of Eigg Heritage Trust and the Knoydart Foundation had been, the SLF was allocated £10.8 million in the first instance and its administration was entrusted to an enlarged Community Land Unit – HIE, in consequence, equipping the CLU with additional staff, some of whom were based at Auchtertyre, in the Lochalsh area of the Highland mainland opposite Skye, where the Scottish Land Fund was launched formally in February 2001.*

One of the CLU's new recruits was Sandra Holmes. Just before the unit's expansion was announced, Sandra had decided to give up a position with Grampian Health Board in Aberdeen in order to take over the management of a family croft at Plockton, not far from Auchteryre. 'I began to buy the *West Highland Free Press* every week in the hope of finding the job I'd need to make it possible for me to live on a small croft from which I was never going to make much, if any, money,' Sandra says. 'I'd made up my mind to apply for every position on offer in or near Lochalsh. Amazingly, the second issue of the *Free Press* I bought in Aberdeen included HIE's advertisement for the posts being created at Auchtertyre. I applied, and I was lucky enough to get the chance to do what I've been doing ever since – helping people find the confidence and the means to get to grips with the management of land and other assets.'

---

* A last declaration of interest. From 1998 until 2004, I was HIE's chairman.

Ask Sandra Holmes what her CLU work has involved and she does not mention long hours, lengthy journeys made often in bad weather, frequent absences from home and all the other drawbacks – as they would seem to most of us – inherent in community development activity in an area like the Highlands and Islands. Instead Sandra talks about the 'inspiring people' it has been her 'privilege to meet'; people 'who give so much for no personal reward'; people whom she has seen 'grow into roles they began by thinking they couldn't possibly take on'. From Sandra Holmes's standpoint, these people have contributed much more to the expansion of community ownership than she, John Watt and their CLU colleagues have done. But in virtually all the localities where community ownership has been established, matters are seen differently. People involved in the management of community-owned land are proud – and rightly so – of their accomplishments. But they could not have got started, many of them insist, if it were not for the assistance and encouragement on offer from HIE's Community Land Unit.

This point is nowhere made more strongly than in Gigha where the CLU, in addition to deploying HIE resources on an unprecedented scale, could draw on the finance made available to the Scottish Land Fund. Although the SLF's advisory committee (appointed just months before) had fixed a grant ceiling of £1 million, the committee, with CLU support, agreed to breach this ceiling in the case of the Isle of Gigha Heritage Trust – the company limited by guarantee which islanders, acting on advice from Simon Fraser, created in order to provide themselves with a properly constituted means of receiving funds and mounting an ownership bid. The heritage trust, it was quickly made known, would be eligible for grant aid of £2.5 million from the Land Fund – together with a loan of a further £1 million. HIE, for its part, promised £500,000 – making £4 million in total. Thus assured of his being able to make a realistic offer for Gigha on behalf of its inhabitants, Simon Fraser – aided by Duncan Baird who had not long before become the CLU's Argyll-based representative – commenced negotiations that concluded, towards the end of October 2001, in the heritage trust's bid being accepted. But as always in such transactions, much detail remained to be sorted out. That was why a formal hand-over of title deeds was delayed until 15 March 2002 – promptly dubbed *Latha Ghiogha* or, in English, Gigha Day. Hence the crowd-

We have placed our full trust in the Gigha community … When we established the Scottish Land Fund earlier this year, we set a normal upper maximum of £1 million for grants from this programme. Because of the exceptional circumstances faced by the community and the absolute necessity that their bid was a strong and realistic one, we went considerably beyond this normal limit in the funding package we made available to the islanders.

Stephen Dunmore, chief executive, New Opportunities Fund, October 2001: West Highland Free Press, 2 November 2001.

We are delighted the islanders of Gigha have been successful … They are following in the footsteps of others, notably Assynt, Eigg and Knoydart, but each community is different and each faces its own challenges … The hard work starts here, but the CLU is prepared to stick around for the long haul and help the islanders realise their dream of a prosperous and confident island.

John Watt, HIE's Community Land Unit, speaking to BBC Scotland, 30 October 2001.

Decades of decline, a succession of private landlords and one *For Sale* sign too many … encouraged us in our quest for change. The 15th of March 2002 was our reward – the day we, as a community, became custodians of our island, the day we took charge of our destiny, the day we bought Gigha.

Friends of Gigha, Membership Leaflet, February 2011.

Last Friday night [15 March 2002] I sat in Gigha's community hall and listened to Willie McSporran, Lorna MacAlister [Gigha's primary school teacher] and Kenny Robison … They spoke of the new dawn on Gigha, their new-found confidence, their hopes and aspirations for the future and, above all, their plans for shaping that new future for themselves and their children. I thought back to the first meeting [seven months before] at which we discussed a community buy-out, and I marvelled at the transformation … At that first meeting, there was no hope, no aspiration, no self-confidence and no plans for the future – just resignation to the fact that, for the third time in twelve years, members of the [Gigha] community were to be bought and sold as millionaires' playthings.

George Lyon MSP, (Liberal Democrat: Argyll and Bute), speaking in the Scottish Parliament, March 2002.

Although we've known since October that our bid to buy the island had succeeded there's no denying that many of us were waiting for this day to come before we believed it was truly happening. However, I think it's also important to say that this is only the beginning of a longer road for us. In the short term we need to raise money, not only to pay what we owe [the Scottish Land Fund], but to provide ourselves with working capital – and we are already actively planning the steps we'll take to secure our longer term future.

Willie McSporran, speaking at the formal handover of Gigha to its residents, 15 March 2002.

pulling proceedings which took place on that date and which resulted in Gigha's ferry crew – who, in the event, coped effortlessly with *Latha Ghiogha*'s bad weather – dealing with a lot more passengers than they had dealt with in a long time.

In medieval Scotland, anyone receiving title to land was handed earth and rock, taken from that land, in a public ceremony – a ceremony which Simon Fraser revived on Gigha when he presented Willie McSporran, not just with documentary proof of the Isle of Gigha Heritage Trust having taken possession of the island, but with a fistful of Gigha soil and a piece of Gigha stone. Thanking Simon and the many others who, he said, had helped bring about what he called his native island's 'new dawn', Willie McSporran commented that, while it was appropriate to celebrate what had been achieved, the heritage trust's purchase of Gigha had been 'the easy part' of a journey on which islanders were just setting out. 'This is only the beginning of a longer road for us,' Willie warned.

The gardens at Achamore House, residence of Gigha's former landlords, are one of the island's visitor attractions and are now in community ownership.

Among the more demanding challenges which Willie McSporran enumerated in the course of the *Latha Ghiogha* celebrations was the requirement to repay – inside two years – the Scottish Land Fund's £1 million loan. The obvious, indeed the only, way to raise the bulk of this sum was by way of property sales. By far the most significant of the ensuing disposals was the sale of Achamore House where – since the mansion's construction in the later nineteenth century – Gigha's landlords had lived when in residence on the island. Although the house's superb gardens (extending to 54 acres) were retained by the heritage trust to ensure that they remained open to the public, the sale of Achamore House (where its new owners launched a tourism business and other ventures) brought in £640,000. Other such transactions could doubtless have closed the remaining gap. But with a view to ensuring that Gigha people proved their commitment to the course they had embarked on, the SLF had stipulated that at least

Carragh an Tairbeirt, the distinctively shaped standing stone which has long been an island landmark and which the Isle of Gigha Heritage Trust incorporated into its logo.

one fifth of its £1 million loan to the Isle of Gigha Heritage Trust had to be repaid from the proceeds of the Gigha community's own fund-raising efforts. Hence the welter of sponsored boat races, sponsored slims, soup-and-sandwich days, quiz nights and associated activities which collectively enabled the heritage trust to repay its borrowed £1 million on schedule in the early part of 2004. This was the first indication of the Isle of Gigha Heritage Trust's ability to get things done. It was not to be the last.

More than half of the forty or so tenanted homes taken over by the heritage trust in 2002 have today been refurbished to a high standard – with others scheduled for renovation. Eighteen new homes for rent have been built on land made available by the trust to Fyne Homes, an Argyll and Bute housing association. And on an island where previous proprietors refused to sell house sites to prospective buyers, a dozen or so privately-owned homes have been constructed on land sold by the community to the homeowners in question.

Developments of this sort have helped bring about a spectacular reversal of the rapid population loss characteristic of pre-2002 Gigha. The total number of island residents, 98 when the heritage trust took charge, is today well over 150 – an increase of almost 60 per cent. Gigha's primary school roll, just six in 2002, is above twenty. And on an island formerly bereft of both twentysomethings and thirtysomethings, there are growing numbers in this economically crucial age group.

Among them is Joe Teale who runs the Boathouse Café Bar – Gigha's equivalent of the Miller sisters' Knoydart tearoom and, like its Knoydart counterpart, an obvious first stop for visitors new off incoming ferries. Joe, with whom it is difficult to snatch more than a word or two on one of the many summer days he spends dealing with customer after customer, is the sort of person who, in the past, would have left Gigha as a teenager – never to return. Now, from premises rented from the Isle of Gigha Heritage Trust and featured during July 2011 in a *Sunday Telegraph* list of Britain's top seaside eating spots, Joe is contributing substantially to the continued expansion of Gigha's economy. He is also enjoying himself. 'I love this place,' Joe Teale says of Gigha.

The Boathouse Café Bar, a five-minute walk from the ferry slip and adjacent to the moorings just off the east coast of [Gigha], was opened in June 2004 to cater for the culinary needs of day-tripper, local, visitor and yachtsman alike. Since then we have been providing anything from a bar snack to a full three-course meal including fresh local seafood … The Boathouse has [also] hosted many nights of entertainment, including nights of contemporary and traditional Scottish music, quiz nights, competitions and private functions.

Boathouse Café Bar website, July 2011.

Highlights? Mussels, lamb, haddock, sticky toffee pudding, friendly smiley service. Drawbacks? We had to be somewhere else next day.

Posting about Boathouse Café Bar on TripAdvisor UK website, July 2011.

Not only the freshest seafood … They also have the most fantastic haggis hotdogs I've ever tasted. One cannot say more.

Contribution to Boathouse Café Bar Facebook Page, July 2011.

The Boathouse Café Bar is one of a dozen or so privately-developed businesses that have sprung up on Gigha as a result of the island's heritage trust having created an enterprise-friendly environment of a type that Gigha's former landlords – perhaps because of their wanting always to be completely in control – refused to countenance. At its own hand, meanwhile, the Isle of Gigha Heritage Trust operates an equally impressive range of income-generating activities. One of the trust's commercial subsidiaries, Gigha Trading Ltd, is in charge of a small quarry, the island's hotel, a number of self-catering cottages and various business premises. A second subsidiary, Gigha Renewable Energy Ltd (GREL), is responsible for the management of Britain's first community-owned and national-grid-connected wind farm – its three turbines, on rising ground towards the south end of the island, visible from the moment one first glimpses Gigha when heading for the Tayinloan ferry terminal.

Those turbines are known in Gigha as *Creideas*, *Dòchas* and *Carthannas* (Faith, Hope and Charity) or 'the dancing ladies'. The affectionate nature of such terms – so different from the epithets hurled at many of the other wind farms installed in the British countryside in recent times – derives from Gigha people's recognition of the gains their turbines have brought them. Unlike Eigg Electric or the Knoydart Foundation, both producing power solely for local consumption, GREL, in the manner of the Assynt Crofters Trust but on a substantially larger scale, sells its energy output to a major utility. By so doing, the company ensures that the Isle of Gigha Heritage Trust can rely on having a significant income stream at its disposal. The 'community benefits' paid annually by the large corporations which control most of the United Kingdom's wind farms amount to some £4,000 per installed megawatt of generating capacity. Since Gigha's wind farm delivers well under one megawatt, islanders might get about £2,500 a year from such an arrangement. By operating its own wind farm on an island which it also owns, the Isle of Gigha Heritage Trust earns between fifty and sixty times as much. This explains why the trust, as noted earlier, is looking to invest in a fourth, and bigger, turbine. It also explains why an island contributor to the heritage trust's website is firmly of the opinion that the dancing ladies 'add to our skyline rather than detracting from it'. But for the revenues provided by *Creideas*, *Dòchas* and *Carthannas*, after all, the Isle of Gigha Heritage Trust would not have been able to deliver either its housing

The Gigha wind [farm] comprises three, pre-commissioned [meaning second-hand] Vestas V27 wind turbines, each with an installed capacity of 225 kilowatts. Each turbine stands on a three-section, 30-metre, rolled steel tower, set on steel reinforced foundations … The turbines are medium-sized by modern standards and whilst they are significant structures … they sit particularly well within the small island landscape.

Energyshare Online Community website, August 2011.

refurbishment programme or the wider – and award-winning – set of improvements which have changed Gigha so greatly for the better.

On the unusually still and warm morning in February 2011 when this book's author last visited Gigha, John Martin, the Isle of Gigha Heritage Trust's vice-chairman took a brief break from the joinery work that keeps him busy even in his seventies. Standing in front of the heritage trust's offices and gesturing in the direction of some of the island's many new homes, John commented: 'If someone had said nine years ago that we'd have achieved as much as we have achieved, I'd have said they were dreaming. What has been realised here on Gigha is far beyond my expectation.' How had he and other islanders found the sheer staying power needed to enable them to do what they have done, I asked. John thought for a bit. 'We have been released from chains,' he said, 'and we have been given the opportunity to be free.'

Susan Allan of the Isle of Gigha Heritage Trust outside the trust's hotel – the first such business in Britain to be taken into community ownership.

The Chartered Institute of Housing Scotland's 2011 Excellence in Regeneration Award ... has gone to the Isle of Gigha Heritage Trust ... The trust's ... partners have included Highlands and Islands Enterprise, and Fyne Homes, [but] it was the commitment, passion and persistence of the trust – and in particular of its volunteer board members – which the judging panel felt had really driven the dramatic turnaround of the island. In 2002, the population numbered 98, with only six children in the primary school. Almost all of the housing stock inherited by the Trust was in awful condition despite being occupied. But the population is now 158, with 22 children in the school, and 23 properties – more than half the total – have been renovated. Employment is up and tourism is very much on the increase. Jim Strang, Chair of CIH Scotland, said: 'The award judges were very much struck by the way in which regeneration has been happening in a steady, incremental way rather than through quick fixes which might not be sustainable in the long term. And it's really worth stressing that the trust has been hugely focused on income generation and has never been able to rely on external funding alone. Creating its own wind farm has provided an income stream which has enabled the trust to borrow money for housing improvement.'

Chartered Institute of Housing Scotland news release, March 2011.

The Isle of Gigha is an example of how serious long-term decline can be reversed. In large part [the island's] success is due to community ownership and all the benefits it has [brought] ... When the combination of community leadership and empowerment ... become available, the results, even in a very small community, can exceed all expectations.

SQW Consulting, **Gigha Community Buy-Out: Five Year Evaluation,** *March 2007.*

———

On Thursday 8 July 1999, exactly a week after the inauguration of Scotland's devolved parliament, and by way of underlining the priority attached to land reform by the Labour-Liberal Democrat coalition which had just taken office in Edinburgh, Jim Wallace, the coalition's senior Liberal Democrat and its Deputy First Minister, launched the new administration's land reform white paper in the little community of Abriachan beside Loch Ness. 'With the ceremonial opening of the new Scottish parliament now out of the way,' commented the Deputy First Minister who was accompanied to Abriachan by two Labour colleagues, 'we can finally get down to the business of taking action on the issues which matter to the people of Scotland. Land reform is clearly one of those issues.'

Abriachan is a scattered rural community of about 140 people set high above the shores of Loch Ness in the Highlands of Scotland … In 1998 the community purchased 534 hectares [1,320 acres] of forest and open hill ground from Forest Enterprise [the Forestry Commission's woodland management wing]. Since then … the Abriachan Forest Trust has managed this land to create local employment, improve the environment and encourage its enjoyment by the public through a network of spectacular paths, family-suited mountain bike trails and innovative education opportunities.

Abriachan Forest Trust website, August 2011.

The proposals thus published by the Scottish Executive, as Scotland's government was known initially, were intended to give effect to recommendations set out six months earlier in the final report of the Land Reform Policy Group. That report had majored on the need to aid and facilitate the expansion of community ownership and this aim was now reiterated by Jim Wallace. The Scottish Executive, he said, intended to introduce legislation which would make it easier for rural communities to take ownership of the land around them. Hence the symbolism inherent in the Deputy First Minister's decision to unveil the executive's reform plans in Abriachan where, more than a year before, local residents – the first group, incidentally, to receive financial help with such a purchase from HIE's Community Land Unit – had bought some 1,300 acres of woodland and hillside from the Forestry Commission.

In Scotland's parliament, land reform had overwhelming support. When, after the period of consultation ushered in by the July 1999 white paper, the Scottish Executive's Land Reform Bill was laid before MSPs in November 2001, it was backed not just by the two coalition parties, Labour and the Liberal Democrats, but by the largest opposition grouping, the SNP – nationalist MSPs generally taking the line that, though an SNP administration would have been more radical, the measure on offer was a welcome step in the right direction. But all land reform – because it

The Scottish Executive's Deputy First Minister, Deputy Justice Minister and Deputy Highlands and Islands Minister – Messrs Jim Wallace, Angus MacKay and Alasdair Morrison respectively – were on parade in Edinburgh on 1 July for the Scottish Parliament's formal opening. Just seven days later, the same trio found themselves in very different surroundings and in different company. Guided by a dozen or so folk from Abriachan, the three ministers were squelching along a muddy track high above Loch Ness. And if the Abriachan people present – ranging in age from eight to eighty – had something of a proprietorial air as they drew the ministerial party's attention to the progress being made in felling and replanting the woodlands fringing the path, this was perfectly excusable. Those woodlands, after all, belong to Abriachan residents. They constitute an example of community ownership in action. Which is why there was something singularly appropriate about Mr Wallace and his colleagues having come to Abriachan to launch the Scottish Executive's land reform white paper.

James Hunter, 'People are key to reform', The Herald, 15 July 1999.

interferes, by definition, with the established order of society – is contentious. Outside parliament, the Land Reform Bill was condemned by landowning interests. Inside parliament, it was attacked vociferously by the Conservative Party. By its Conservative critics, notably Bill Aitken, a Glasgow MSP, the planned legislation was portrayed as Marxist in inspiration – Aitken taking particular exception to legislative provisions intended to promote community ownership. These provisions, Bill Aitken said in the course of 2002 and 2003 were 'a disgrace'. They amounted to a 'land-grab' of which the Zimbabwean dictator Robert Mugabe (them presiding over the seizure of his country's white-owned farms) would have been proud. They were an 'expropriation of property' which would 'lead to the destruction [of] smaller rural communities' and bring about a widespread 'loss of jobs'. This was to exaggerate wildly – as subsequent developments were to show – the Land Reform Bill's potential impact. It was also to ignore already accumulating evidence from places like Assynt, Eigg, Knoydart and

There is no doubt that communities across Scotland want to take more control over the management and use of the land on which they live and work. There is a widespread agreement that an overhaul of the pattern of land ownership in our country is long overdue. We very much hope that the Bill results in a significant change in the pattern of land ownership in Scotland … Other countries have taken far more radical steps than Scotland will do today … The Tories should be warned that much more radical measures could have been proposed … As far as the SNP is concerned, the Bill may not be perfect, but it has our support.

Roseanna Cunningham MSP, (SNP: Perth), speaking in the Scottish parliament on the day, 23 January 2003, the Land Reform Bill was passed.

One of the many buildings renovated by the Isle of Gigha Heritage Trust.

Gigha that, far from accelerating rural depopulation and reducing rural employment opportunities, community ownership was having exactly the opposite effect – as anticipated by other Tories, Russell Sanderson and Michael Forsyth, who, when fostering the intial spread of community ownership in the Highlands and Islands during the 1990s, had thought its likely outcomes to be perfectly compatible with Conservative thinking.

The Land Reform Bill, to be fair to Bill Aitken, was meant to empower communities in ways that neither Forsyth nor Sanderson had been prepared to contemplate. As eventually enacted, the Scottish Executive's reform measures – with consequences explored later – enabled crofting communities to buy croft land from owners who wished to retain it. Non-crofting communities, whether in the Highlands and Islands or in the rest of rural Scotland, received no such entitlement. But they were provided with an opportunity to register an interest in land in their vicinity in order to ensure that, if the land in which interest was thus expressed came on the market, the community which had recorded its interest in it would become, in effect, this land's preferred purchaser – as long as the community in question could raise the land's purchase price within six months.

This is undoubtedly a dark day for the Scottish parliament. The Bill has nothing to do with land reform and everything to do with the other parties in the parliament being obsessed with replaying the class wars of 200 years ago. It is an extreme measure, as was well articulated by Roseanna Cunningham, who indicated exactly what more extreme measures might be forthcoming in the unlikely event of the Scottish nationalists ever gaining control of Scotland … Frankly, the Bill is a disgrace. If it is voted through, this will be a day of shame.

Bill Aitken MSP, (Conservative: Glasgow), speaking in the Scottish parliament on the day, 23 January 2003, the Land Reform Bill was passed.

The narrow, concentrated and often absentee pattern of land ownership is failing rural Scotland … Of course there are exceptions: there are good landlords who … have their community's interests close to their hearts. However, I reject the proposition, which has been expressed by the Tories and other opponents of land reform, that rural development in modern Scotland should be predicated on whether people are lucky enough to have a good landlord. That is arrant nonsense … The Liberal Democrat and Labour parties believe fundamentally that wider land ownership is a good thing. We believe that it will be a spur to rural development and that it will create jobs and opportunities for all who live and work on Scotland's land. The most important point is that the Bill seeks to empower people and give them responsibility for their destiny.

George Lyon MSP, (Liberal Democrat: Argyll and Bute), speaking in the Scottish parliament on the day, 23 January 2003, the Land Reform Bill was passed.

The pattern of land ownership in the Highlands and Islands today is not a harmless relic from a bygone age … That pattern of ownership represents a serious distortion of our social and economic life and the time has finally come to consign it to history. Today we are lighting a beacon for radical and sweeping land reform right across the Highlands.

Alasdair Morrison MSP, (Labour: Western Isles), speaking in the Scottish parliament on the day, 23 January 2003, the Land Reform Bill was passed.

———

In the spring of 2002, shortly after community ownership was established in Gigha and with the Land Reform Bill still trundling through the Scottish parliament, the North Harris Estate was advertised for sale. Its 55,000 acres had once belonged, like the rest of Harris and Lewis, to Lord Leverhulme. Subsequently, the estate experienced, like so many similar properties, a prolonged sequence of ownership changes. Its proprietors – most of them attracted by North Harris's superb salmon and sea trout fishing – included, for two years in the 1940s, Lord Brocket (of Knoydart infamy) who was succeeded by Sir Thomas Sopwith, an aircraft manufacturer. Sopwith's sale of North Harris in 1961 was followed, just seven years later, by a further sale – the purchaser this time being a Nottinghamshire landowner, Sir Hereward Wake, who claimed descent from the eleventh-century Fenland outlaw of the same name. Sir Hereward's opinion of his Hebridean tenantry can be deduced from his having tried to persuade Inverness-shire County Council, then the relevant local authority, to reroute the public road in front of Amhuinnsuidhe Castle – on the grounds that it would be helpful (Amhuinnsuidhe serving as Sir Hereward's home when he visited Harris) if island road-users, instead of spoiling their laird's view of the sea, were kept well to the castle's rear where they would be out of his sight. The council, dominated at the time by other landlords, would have done as requested had not the then recently

North Harris lies seventeen miles off the north-western tip of Skye in the Outer Hebrides … The [North Harris] Estate … features a unique combination of sandy beaches, mountains, rugged coastlines and numerous freshwater lochans. The area is also a fantastic place for watching wildlife and boasts a rich cultural history … With around 700 inhabitants, North Harris is sparsely populated. Approximately half the population live in Tarbert, the largest settlement, with the remainder living in small crofting townships scattered along the coastline … The North Harris Trust, which manages the land on behalf of the community, is open to all residents and is run by a board of locally elected volunteer directors. The Trust aims to increase employment opportunities, address local housing needs, and protect and enhance North Harris's wonderful cultural and natural heritage.

North Harris Trust website, August 2011.

established *West Highland Free Press* so effectively rubbished the scheme as to cause its abandonment – an outcome which doubtless contributed to Sir Hereward Wake's subsequent decision to put North Harris up for sale once again.

The estate's next buyer, in 1976, was Gerald Panchaud, a Swiss businessman whose landholding company, despite its having a Lausanne address, was incorporated in Panama. Panchaud, who also owned the 61,000 acre Mar Lodge Estate on Deeside and the 15,000 acre Tulchan Estate in Moray, was one of the overseas purchasers of Scottish landed properties whose activities so exercised the SNP of this period. Some of these purchasers were out and out speculators – notably the Dutch cattle dealer, Johannes Hellinga, who bought and resold extensive acreages in Skye, Easter Ross and Sutherland before becoming one more of the Highlands and Islands lairds whose careers have ended in their imprisonment. Panchaud, or so he insisted, had no speculative intentions. But this most certainly could not be said of Nazmudin Virani, to whom Panchaud sold the 2,500 acre island of Scarp, off North Harris's Atlantic coast. Virani was managing director of the Control Securities property group, one of the fastest growing such concerns in Britain during the 1980s. It was his company's intention, he announced, to equip Scarp with '150 traditional-style Highland cottages to be used as holiday homes' – occupiers of these homes to have exclusive use of 'a landing strip for private planes' and 'a luxury sports complex' comprising 'a swimming pool, a sauna, a solarium, squash courts and all-weather tennis courts'. Perhaps needless to say, nothing whatsoever came of this and Virani, like Hellinga, was eventually jailed – as a result, in Virani's case, of his role in concealing from its auditors the mounting financial troubles of a bank that was shortly afterwards to collapse into insolvency.*

Gerald Panchaud died in 1992 and in 1994 his widow sold the North Harris Estate to Jonathan Bulmer whose wealth derived from his substantial stake in the cider-

---

* This was the Bank of Credit and Commerce International in which, as it happened, Western Isles Council, the local authority in charge of Harris and the rest of the Outer Hebrides from the mid-1970s, deposited £24 million just prior to the bank going bust in July 1991.

producing company of the same name. Bulmer, North Harris's seventh proprietor in half a century, was to be one of the many Highlands and Islands landlords to come and go inside a decade. In April 2002 he made known he was selling the North Harris Estate – his asking price being £4.5 million.

Jonathan Bulmer, who lived permanently at Amhuinnsuidhe (instead of using the castle as a holiday home) and whose children attended the local school, was easily the most popular laird (the competition, admittedly, not being fierce) North Harris had had in a long time. But the ownership history of the estate was such as to cause a great deal of anxiety as to who might take his place. Within days of the property's sale being publicised, therefore, a public meeting was held to discuss prospects for a community bid. Among the people invited to this meeting were John Watt and Sandra Holmes of HIE's Community Land Unit – accompanied,

An exceptional residential and sporting estate possessing some of the finest salmon and sea trout fishing in the country.

Knight Frank, **The Amhuinnsuidhe and North Harris Estate: Sale Particulars,** *April 2002.*

From the low tide of the sea ... A beach on North Harris's Atlantic coast.

We felt we had a consensus … to go forward and look at the proposal [of a community purchase] seriously. We have to look at it. We may never get the chance again.

Kenny MacKay, chairman, North Harris Community Steering Group, May 2002: West Highland Free Press, 17 May 2002.

as John had been at the comparable gathering in Gigha, by Simon Fraser whose unmatched understanding of the legal and financial complexities in the way of achieving community ownership was making his advice indispensable on all such occasions. Although many more meetings were to be called before North Harris's future was settled, this first one resulted in agreement that the locality's residents should set out on what was beginning to be a familiar path – involving, at an early stage, the election of a steering group whose members, aided both by Simon Fraser and by Sandra Holmes, were to spend several months working out exactly how they should proceed.

Although Jonathan Bulmer – who thus demonstrated why he was well regarded in Harris – promised the steering group 'a sympathetic hearing', he was constrained by his having earlier decided to vest ownership of the North Harris Estate in a trust whose beneficiaries were his family and whose trustees were legally obliged to maximise returns to those beneficiaries. There would, then, be no easily-clinched deal on offer. And if financial backing for a community bid was to be got from the Scottish Land Fund and from Highlands and Islands Enterprise, two stipulations had to be met: residents had to be strongly supportive of their taking control of the North Harris Estate; and such control, if proceeded with, needed to be on a basis that would deliver long-run financial viability. The first of these conditions was fulfilled by a September 2002 ballot which, on a turn-out of nearly 75 per cent, delivered a three-to-one majority in favour of attempting a community buy-out. This provided the North Harris Trust, formally constituted that same month, with the mandate needed for a bid. But for all that the trust's newly elected directors were convinced they could make a go of managing the North Harris Estate's 55,000 acres, they were worried about the financial implications of their also trying to acquire Amhuinnsuidhe Castle and its associated salmon fishings. Together these accounted for more than half the £4.5 million being demanded by the North Harris Estate's selling agents. And it was by no means clear how either the castle or the fishings could be run at a profit by the North Harris community. Hence the significance of the deal the North Harris Trust now made with the Stoke-on-Trent businessman whose co-operation with the trust was to guarantee its success.

The ballot result in North Harris represents a triumph of good sense and hope for the future over the sense of caution which is inherent in island communities. Above all perhaps, it is a tribute to the leadership which has been shown within the community itself … The work of the North Harris Community Steering Group has been exceptional. They have … made no grandiose assumptions about what the community might go along with. Hearts and minds have been won because they have been argued for on a rational and reasonable basis … This makes the outcome of the ballot all the more significant. It is a thoughtful vote about how the place can help itself in future and the role that land can play in that process. It is … a vote … in favour of a future in which people can play a greater part in shaping their own destiny.

West Highland Free Press *editorial, 20 September 2002.*

The steering group are of the unanimous view that one option stands out from others in the [feasibility] study [the group has conducted]. This involves the purchase of part of the estate – excluding the castle and the fishings. This option is affordable [and] without financial risk to the community.

North Harris Community Steering Group, letter to North Harris residents, September 2002.

The businessman in question was Ian Scarr-Hall, head of the GSH Group, a company managing electrical and mechanical facilities at some 35,000 sites worldwide. Harris had been known to Scarr-Hall since he first went there as a boy. He aimed to make community ownership of the North Harris Estate a more feasible proposition than it might otherwise have been by allying himself with the North Harris Trust, which had been contemplating a bid for just part of the property, in a jointly mounted offer for the estate in its entirety. As a result of his many visits to Harris, Ian Scarr-Hall said by way of explaining his role in what happened next, he had learned something of the island's history and of how, since the extensive clearances Harris had experienced in the nineteenth century, its people, and especially the crofting families among them, had often been obliged to endure 'conditions of extreme hardship'. Until the emergence of the community ownership movement, the GSH president went on, it had been 'impossible to conceive' that the crofting and other residents of North Harris 'could ever become landowners with responsibility for their own … destiny'. Now that such a possibility was within reach, Ian Scarr-Hall continued, he saw it 'as a great privilege to be a participant in this historic achievement'.

North Harris Estate.

After thorough discussion with potential partners … the North Harris Trust are very happy to advise that we have now agreed to co-operate with Mr Ian Scarr-Hall with a view to presenting an offer for the North Harris Estate in its entirety. We feel confident that we have found a partner who shares the same aims and objectives as ourselves. Ian Scarr-Hall has had connections with Harris for many years, is familiar with the estate and is known by local people. He has contributed personally to several Harris causes, particularly in the voluntary sector, and we are now looking forward to working with him in a business capacity.

North Harris Trust news release, October 2002.

By the end of 2002, Ian Scarr-Hall and the North Harris Trust had secured the North Harris Estate; the former taking ownership of Amhuinnsuidhe Castle and its fishings; the latter assuming responsibility for all the other assets that had been up for sale. The trust's share of the total purchase price was £2.2 million. Of this amount, £1.6 million came from the Scottish Land Fund and £400,000 from HIE's Community Land Unit. The John Muir Trust, because much of the land area of North Harris consists of exactly the sort of terrain JMT wants conserved and protected, contributed £100,000 in return for its becoming involved in North Harris in much the same way as the organisation was already involved in Knoydart. That left a further £100,000 to find – the bulk of it coming from community fund-raising of the sort then still going on in Gigha.

In the course of the congratulatory message he sent to David Cameron, the local businessman who served as the interim chair of the North Harris Trust and who had a key role in the trust's negotiations with Jonathan Bulmer and his representatives, Gigha's Willie McSporran wrote: 'Since any of us can remember, the destinies of our communities have lain in the hands of others. This is no more. We now have the authority to plan our own path, to make our own way.'

This authority, as Willie called it, was acquired formally in Harris on Friday 21 March 2003 when Simon Fraser, doing as he had done in Gigha a year before, handed David Cameron earth and stone taken from what thus became the North Harris Trust's estate. 'For the first time,' David said, 'the people of North Harris can look at their land and know that it belongs to them. We now have so many opportunities that can benefit not just us but all the generations to come.'

Top: *Alasdair MacLeod, the North Harris Trust's development manager.*

Bottom: *Steven Morrison, one of the North Harris Trust's staff team.*

David Cameron, island businessman and a key figure in the establishment of community ownership in North Harris.

The 55,000 acre North Harris Estate was put up for sale unexpectedly at the end of April 2002, just six months after the Highlands and Islands Enterprise network had assisted the inhabitants of Gigha with a successful bid for their island … It was clear that another major opportunity for a community to acquire its land was in prospect. When a private buyer with local connections began to show interest in acquiring elements of the estate … we helped the newly formed North Harris Trust to put together an innovative public/private bid … This approach proved successful. Businessman Ian Scarr-Hall bought Amhuinnsuidhe Castle and associated fishing rights while the residents of North Harris, through the trust, gained the remainder of the estate.

Highlands and Islands Enterprise, Annual Report, June 2003.

The John Muir Trust is the only external representative on the North Harris Trust's board of directors. We are fully committed to helping the community … to manage, develop and conserve the assets of the North Harris estate in a sustainable manner for the benefit of the community and the enjoyment of the wider public.

John Muir Trust website, August 2011.

Since any of us can remember, the destinies of our communities have lain in the hands of others. This is no more. We now have the authority to plan our own path, to make our own way. On Saturday [the first anniversary of the Isle of Gigha Heritage Trust taking charge of Gigha] we likened our island's development under community ownership to the growth of a tree. Already we can see the flowering buds, but it will be in future years that we will see the full fruits.

Willie McSporran, chairman, Isle of Gigha Heritage Trust, in a congratulatory message to the community of North Harris, March 2003.

From time immemorial it was the custom and the law of Scotland that, when a new owner was given possession of land, this would be done in a ceremony held on the land itself. In this ceremony, in the presence of witnesses, stone and earth of that land would be handed to the new owner. This ceremony was known as giving sasine. An account of the ceremony was written down in Latin and that account recorded in a Register of Sasines. Through time the recording of the written account became more important, and eventually the ceremony of sasine was abolished. However, it was revived in Gigha last year and we are now going to bring it back to the Western Isles.

I now call on David Cameron to receive sasine on behalf of the North Harris Trust.

David Cameron, I hereby deliver into your hands stone and earth of this land, and in so doing give unto the North Harris Trust true and lawful sasine of these whole lands of North Harris, from the low tide of the sea to the highest mountain tops, *a coelo usque ad centrum*, to be held on behalf of the people of North Harris in all time coming; *agus tha sinn uile a tha cruinn còmhla an seo an dràsda a' guidhe gu soirbhich leibh agus leis gach ginealach a tha ri teachd agus gum faigh sibh a h-uile beannachd anns an talamh seo a tha ar Tighearna air a thoirt dhuibh ri shealbhachadh.*

All we who are gathered together at this moment pray that you and every generation to come will prosper, and that you will receive every blessing on this land which our Lord has given you to enjoy.

Simon Fraser, solicitor, Stornoway, at the formal hand-over of the North Harris Estate to the North Harris Trust, March 2003.

Until recently, it was a prospect which did not even feature in our dreams and aspirations. North Harris was a bastion that would never crumble; a symbol of Hebridean landlordism ... If anyone doubts that the trickle of land reform in the Highlands is going to become a tide, then they should observe what has happened in North Harris over the past few months. Ownership and management of these estates by the people who live on them is a noble concept whose time has come.

Brian Wilson MP, Minister of State for Energy, March 2003: West Highland Free Press, 28 March 2003.

The Bhaltos Peninsula, the area of the Bhaltos Estate, has always been a rich, densely settled part of the Isle of Lewis … When the opportunity arose for buying the Bhaltos Estate from the [then] landlord, James Gilchrist, a steering group was set up in November 1998 with a remit to form a company which could purchase and manage the estate … for the benefit of the whole community … The Bhaltos Estate totals 690 hectares [1,700 acres] … The estate covers a variety of terrain, from rocky moorland to machair and shore. There are five [crofting] villages [or townships] within the estate.

Bhaltos Community Trust website, August 2011.

What had been a 'trickle of land reform,' Brian Wilson predicted in March 2003, 'is going to become a tide.' Although progress has been slower elsewhere, this certainly proved true of the Outer Hebrides, the chain of islands stretching through the 130 miles – north to south – separating the Butt of Lewis from Barra Head. By the close of the twenty-first century's first decade, well over half the land surface of the Western Isles, the island group's other designation, was in community ownership. This means that more than three-quarters of all the people living in the Outer Hebrides live today on land they themselves own collectively. That is remarkable. In under ten years, an ownership pattern which appeared to be forever fixed had been changed in a manner little short of revolutionary.

The first small segment of the Outer Hebrides to go into community ownership since the establishment of the Stornoway Trust in 1923 was the Bhaltos Estate on the western edge of Lewis. In 1998, its proprietor, James Gilchrist, a Glasgow architect, announced, first, that he was selling the estate and, second, that his preferred buyer was the local community – Bhaltos residents taking over at the start of 1999. 'It's up to you now to make [Bhaltos] a success,' James Gilchrist told them.

When set alongside the Stornoway Trust's 70,000 acres, the Bhaltos Estate's 1,700 acres did not add significantly to the percentage of Outer Isles land in community control. But the overall total was increased greatly by the success of the North Harris Trust and boosted further when, in 2006, residents of the Seaforth Estate, in the north-eastern corner of Harris, voted both to buy the property and to join forces with their North Harris neighbours. This took the area held by the North Harris Trust to some 63,000 acres and, at the same time, restored the North Harris Estate to its original dimensions – the Seaforth Estate (previously part of the North Harris property) having existed only since 1994 when Helen Panchaud, then selling the bulk of her late husband's Harris landholdings to Jonathan Bulmer, kept this part of these landholdings in her possession.

In Lewis, meanwhile, the focus of attention had shifted to the Galson Estate in the most northerly part of the island. In 1924 its 56,000 acres had been disposed of by

Lord Leverhulme for just £500 – an astonishingly tiny sum (even by the standards of an economically depressed era) in that the property's purchaser was charged well under a pound for every hundred acres he acquired. Eighty years later, three descendants of this purchaser were the sole directors of Galson Estate Ltd, the company in which the estate's ownership had been vested for much of the intervening period. Almost all of the Galson Estate was in crofting tenure. This meant (crofting families of the sort constituting the bulk of the estate's 2,000 or so occupants having had security of tenure since 1886) there was no risk of Galson Estate Ltd's tenants being ejected from their homes – as had seemed likely to happen to their Gigha counterparts in the wake of Malcolm Potier's 1991 bankruptcy. But in 2004, when moves to take Galson Estate into community ownership got underway, there were real worries among local residents that, their crofting rights notwithstanding, they were losing control of what was going on around them. This was because of developments planned by Lewis Wind Power, a company set up jointly by two generating corporations, AMEC and British Energy, with a view to this company constructing 234 very large wind turbines in the northern half of Lewis – many of them on sites adjacent to the Galson Estate's twenty-two crofting townships.

Residents of these townships felt themselves excluded from, and in the dark about, the various deals being negotiated by Lewis Wind Power (LWP) with Galson Estate Ltd. But the Scottish Executive's Land Reform Act, which came into force in 2004, enabled them to change this situation – the Act, as indicated earlier, providing people living on crofting properties with an absolute right to bring these properties into community ownership. Would the Galson Estate's population have chosen to exercise this right, or to exercise it so quickly, in the absence of the unsettling impact of Lewis Wind Power's proposals? That is unclear. What is certain, however, is that hostility to these proposals helped to maximise backing from crofters and others for a community ownership bid. After all, such ownership, if it could be brought about, was bound to give Galson Estate residents a greater say in what happened next in their part of Lewis. And had LWP's wind farm gone ahead – which, in the event, it did not – ownership would have ensured that people in the vicinity of its turbines got greater financial benefits from them than would otherwise have been the case.

Butt of Lewis lighthouse at the northern extremity of the Galson Estate. The next land sighted by a west-bound ship is in Canada.

But if anti-LWP feeling was one factor in the support gained by the newly formed Urras Oighreachd Ghabhsainn (UOG), or Galson Estate Trust, during the summer and early autumn of 2004, it was by no means the only such factor. Another, as so often in the community ownership story, is to be found in many estate residents' strong sense of their locality's history and their consequent awareness that, in rallying behind UOG's purchase plans, they were, in some way, aligning themselves with those of their forebears who had suffered eviction but had also – despite the risks of so doing – spoken out against clearance and its perpetrators.

When, in June 1883, members of the royal commission then enquiring into crofting grievances came to the Galson area, they heard a great deal about the evictions that had occurred between twenty and forty years before – evictions culminating in several townships being emptied of people to make way for the sheep-rearing enterprise known as Galson Farm. At one of the public meetings called by Urras Oighreachd Ghabhsainn, extracts from the testimony given by Lewis delegates to the 1883 commission were read aloud by Agnes Rennie, a Galson Estate resident who was active in the Urras from the start and is today the organisation's chair. These readings included words first spoken by John Macdonald, a crofter then living in North Dell – one of the townships UOG intended, more than 120 years later, to bring into community ownership. 'Do you know about the people who were removed from Galson [Farm]?' Macdonald was asked. 'I ought to,' he replied. 'I was born there.' His family was one

of more than a hundred affected by this particular clearance, John Macdonald went on. Questioned further, he provided additional details; and not least because of the matter-of-fact way he did so, says Agnes Rennie who manages a Lewis-based publishing company, Macdonald's remarks retain their original force. 'At the close of the meeting at which I read out John Macdonald's words,' Agnes recalls, 'a lot of people came up to me to say how much they'd been affected by their having heard what he had had to say.'

But if men like John Macdonald made history in the 1880s, when the Highland Land League's ultimately successful struggle for security of tenure was at its height, Agnes Rennie and her colleagues were making history too. In attempting to take over the Galson Estate – which its owners had neither put on the market nor had any intention of so doing – Urras Oighreachd Ghabhsainn's members, soon many hundreds strong, were doing something nobody had attempted, or could have attempted, before.

Agnes Rennie of Urras Oighreachd Ghabhsainn, the Galson Trust.

Individual crofters, as mentioned previously, have been entitled to buy their crofts – with or without the blessing of their landlords – since 1976. The provisions of Michael Forsyth's Transfer of Crofting Estates Act, as also mentioned previously, had

Facing page, left: *One of the many crofting townships constituting the Galson Estate.* **Right:** *Ness Post Office on the Galson Estate.*

Q. Do you know about the people who were removed from Galson [Farm]?

A. I ought to. I was born there, and my ancestors lived there.

Q. What was the name of the town[ship] you lived in?

A. North Galson.

Q. How many families were removed from that town[ship]?

A. There were over sixty of them …

Q. Were there any more townships cleared beside North Galson?

A. [An]other three.

Q. Name them.

A. Balmeanach, Melbost and South Galson. In Balmeanach there were ten families, in Melbost twenty-five, and in South Galson thirteen …

Q. There seem to have been 108 families altogether – we shall say upwards of 100. What became of these families?

A. About forty of them went to America. The rest were scattered all over the country.

John Macdonald, crofter, South Dell, giving evidence to the Commissioners of Inquiry into the Condition of the Crofters and Cottars in the Highlands and Islands of Scotland, June 1883.

extended this right-to-buy to groups of crofting tenants on state-owned land – any set of such crofters being able, from 1997 onwards and at a point of their choosing, to take collective possession of croft land in their vicinity. But for all that Michael Forsyth had been happy to transfer land in crofting tenure from a public body to its occupants, and for all that he had been equally happy to encourage the proprietors of privately-owned crofting estates to make similar transfers, the pre-1997 Conservative government had refused to place landlords (other than the government's own agricultural department) under a legally-enforceable obligation to make croft land available for community purchase. Post-1997 administrations, however, took a different line. The UK Labour government's Land Reform Policy Group called for legislation which would 'give to all other crofting communities the same basic rights to acquire their croft land' as had been made available to the state's crofting tenants 'through the provision of the Transfer of Crofting Estates Act.' Having being accepted by Scotland's first devolved administration, this recommendation was given effect by the Land Reform Act of 2003. Hence Urras Oighreachd Ghabhsainn's ability – its plans endorsed comprehensively in the now standard local ballot – to initiate a process intended to culminate in Galson Estate Ltd being obliged to sell its 56,000 acres to UOG and its members.

The directors of Galson Estate Ltd (none of whom lived locally but all of whom lived elsewhere in Lewis) had nothing in common with lairds of the sort who had engendered so much resentment in places like Eigg and Knoydart. Indeed Norman Thomson, who was elected UOG's first chairman soon after he came home to Lewis at the end of a career in the oil industry, believes that some Galson Estate residents were a little reluctant, at the outset, to move against landlords whose profile, prior to Lewis Wind Power coming on the scene, could scarcely have been lower: 'People were inclined to say the estate's owners had never done us any harm. But against that was the

Legislation [is required] to give all crofting communities ... a right to have ownership of their croft land ... on fair financial terms. This legislation will aim to give to all other crofting communities the same basic rights to acquire their croft land as are already available to the Secretary of State [for Scotland]'s croft tenants through the provisions of the Transfer of Crofting Estates (Scotland) Act 1997.

Land Reform Policy Group, Recommendations for Action, January 1999.

A cultural centre on the Galson Estate.

The Land Reform (Scotland) Act 2003 has three main components. Part 1 introduced new rights of access ... Part 2 provided a right to buy for local communities [in all of rural Scotland] ... Part 3 introduced a right-to-buy for crofting communities. Under Part 2, local community bodies in rural Scotland can apply to Scottish ministers to register an interest in rural land ... A community then has the right of first refusal when that land is sold ... The crofting right to buy is far more radical because the initiative rests with the purchaser. If a crofting community chooses to exercise its right to buy croft land, the landowner is forced to sell it ... This constitutes a dramatic extension and change of the right-to-buy which individual crofters have had since 1976.

Charles Warren, Managing Scotland's Environment, *Edinburgh University Press, 2009.*

fact that they hadn't done us much, if any, good either.' This was unarguable. Galson Estate Ltd did not employ anyone and had not engaged in any developmental activity. If Urras Oighreachd Ghabhsainn managed to get hold of the Galson Estate and create even one or two jobs in the ensuing four or five years, then, it would have contributed more to the locality's economy than Galson Estate Ltd had contributed in decades. First, however, Norman Thomson and UOG's other directors had to find their way through legislation which, though it ostensibly entitled them to purchase the land on which they lived, could scarcely have been more hedged about by complexity.

As this book's concluding chapter will contend, the crofting right-to-buy provisions of the 2003 Land Reform Act involve so many time-consuming and expensive procedures as to make this aspect of the Act next best to valueless. From an Urras Oighreachd Ghabhsainn perspective, therefore, it was as well that Galson Estate's

Members of Urras Oighreachd Ghabsainn (Galson Trust) at the Butt of Lewis lighthouse. Left to right: James Macleod, Carola Bell, Donald Macleod and Norman Thomson.

proprietors, rather than battle on as they might have done for many years, consented to sell to UOG at a mutually agreed price. On 12 January 2007, at a ceremony staged appropriately enough at Galson Farm, Urras Oighreachd Ghabhsainn accordingly became the latest community group to assume ownership of a large area of land.

In an age when communities are becoming increasingly dislocated, there is something inherently right about the people of these islands taking responsibility for the land. It is the most precious resource we have; it is our most tangible legacy from the past; and we have a duty to cherish it for future generations.

Agnes Rennie, Urras Oighreachd Ghabhsainn, January 2007: **West Highland Free Press,** *19 January 2007.*

Friday 12 January 2007 will be remembered as a historic day for the community of Galson Estate ... On this day the 56,000 acre estate passed into community ownership ... The celebrations began at Galson Farm, a location closely associated with the tumultuous events of the nineteenth century in this area ... People gathered in the yard, despite [a] storm, to witness this momentous occasion, and when the pipes skirled a loud cheer went up to acknowledge [that] the land now belonged to the people.

The Crofter, *the news magazine of the Scottish Crofting Foundation, February 2007.*

The Galson area's way of life is about the intricate interaction between a crofting lifestyle, a panoramic landscape and a diverse natural environment. The area boasts fantastic coastal scenery and white sands; large Special Areas of Conservation and Special Protection Areas; a variety of flora and fauna including golden eagles, fulmars and gannets; excellent sea and fresh water fishing; and, most importantly, a kindly, 'down-to-earth' community that works together to bring about a better future for themselves and future generations.

Urras Oighreachd Ghabhsainn website, August 2011.

In one of his best known poems, 'A Man in Assynt', published more than twenty years before the Assynt Crofters Trust existed, Norman MacCaig, who knew Assynt intimately, asked who owned this crofting district's mountain landscape: 'The millionaire who bought it or the poacher staggering downhill in the early morning with a deer on his back?' Much the same question could have been asked of North

From the early days of community ownership, members of the community were keen to have the opportunity to stalk in North Harris. In order to involve the community in deer management the [North Harris] Trust facilitated the establishment of the Harris Stalking Club in 2004. The club is open to anyone living in Harris or the South Lochs area of Lewis and is run by its members as a separate body from the trust. The club has been a considerable success and currently has 25 members, 15 of whom have been trained to Deer Stalking Certificate Level One in stalking best-practice methods and deer biology. Members of the stalking club now carry out most of the hind [female deer] stalking, enabling members to enjoy the sport and the trust to manage its deer herd successfully.

North Harris Trust website, August 2011.

Harris, a locality MacCaig also knew well and one, like Assynt, that belonged for a long time to men whose interest in acquiring such places derived principally from their wishing to possess, over substantial slabs of wild country, an exclusive entitlement to fish for salmon and an equally exclusive entitlement to shoot red deer. To be a poacher in such circumstances was to strike a blow – and to be seen to strike a blow – against an ownership structure thought unacceptable by the many people in the Highlands and Islands who, irrespective of what the law might say, find it hard to accept that anyone should have property rights in wild creatures.

If you are of this deeply-held opinion, there is a certain satisfaction to be got from the North Harris Trust having set up a deer stalking club – its membership consisting entirely of local residents. The club was made possible by the manner in which the North Harris Estate was divided between the trust and Ian Scarr-Hall in 2003. Although the latter (with, as stressed earlier, the North Harris Trust's strong backing) took charge of the estate's salmon fishings, management of its red deer herd, numbering well over a thousand animals, became a trust responsibility. Because the North Harris Trust is committed to expanding native woodland and otherwise enhancing and conserving the North Harris landscape, such management requires deer numbers to be kept in check. This is done by the stalking club. 'Members pay a small annual membership fee,' says North Harris Trust chairman Calum MacKay. 'They've taken a number of training courses. They've made themselves expert deer managers and, by the way, they're death on poachers.' Asked if some Harris Stalking Club members – as does not seem wholly improbable – might once have been poachers themselves, Calum looks quizzically at Iain MacSween, one of his North Harris Trust colleagues who is sitting on the other side of the Harris Hotel table around which this conversation is taking place. Iain grins and shakes his head. 'No comment,' he says firmly.

Managing deer, planting trees and upgrading North Harris's badly neglected network of paths and tracks are among the several environmental improvements being put into effect by the North Harris Trust in close collaboration with its partner organisation, the John Muir Trust. But important though these activities are, they by no means monopolise the North Harris Trust's attentions. 'It's every ownership group's most basic task to do whatever can be done to improve living conditions in the communities we're here to serve,' says David Cameron who had a key role in the North Harris Trust and who, as Community Land Scotland's chairman, now answers to the wider community ownership movement. 'Environmental enhancement is an important part of that job. But it can't be the only part. Our communities need more and better housing. They need more and better jobs. We have to be seen to be providing these.'

Both in North Harris and on Lewis's Galson Estate there is widespread agreement with the CLS chairman's analysis of what the community owners of the two areas have somehow to deliver. A Gigha-style collaboration between the North Harris Trust and a local housing association has resulted in eight new homes being made available at affordable rents. Fully-serviced house sites are on offer to private buyers from the same trust which is also, like its Galson counterpart, promoting tourism,

Although … [the] North Harris [Estate] appears almost completely devoid of native woodland, an exploration of gullies, crags and islands will reveal a number of native tree species clinging on in areas that sheep and deer cannot reach. The most common species is rowan, but there is also a scatter of aspen, holly and several species of willow … Following [its] purchase of the estate the [North Harris] Trust has been working to increase the amount of woodland on North Harris, with the aim of creating a network of woodland habitats across the estate.

North Harris Trust website, August 2011.

One of South Uist's many freshwater lochs.

generating renewable energy, constructing business premises and otherwise looking to boost employment prospects. That last task has been made a little easier in the North Harris case because of Ian Scarr-Hall's GSH Group having decided to conduct some of its worldwide operations from Tarbert, North Harris's principal settlement. This has resulted in more than twenty new jobs being created in an area where such jobs have long been rare. 'But more jobs are needed,' David Cameron insists, 'if we're to reverse population outflows that have been going on for generations.'

Not far from the North Harris Trust's Tarbert offices, an identical message is to be heard from Neil Campbell and other directors of the West Harris Trust which, as recounted earlier, gained possession of the Borve, Luskentyre and Scaristavore Estates in 2010. Take the ferry from Harris to the Uists, a more southerly subdivision of the Outer Isles, and the same determination to make community land ownership a means of generating economic growth is evident in the work of Stòras Uibhist, the community land trust which bought the South Uist Estate in 2006.

Stòras Uibhist's chairman is Angus MacMillan, a local businessman and very much the organisation's driving force. Born and brought up in South Uist, Angus, in accordance with a long-established pattern, left as a teenager for the mainland where he trained as an engineer. Most young people who quit the Outer Isles in this way do not return. But Angus did – taking a local authority job initially and then setting up a fish-farming enterprise which he managed successfully for many years.

'The beginnings of Stòras Uibhist can be traced back to the mid-1990s,' Angus says. Much the biggest employer in the area then was the UK government's Ministry of Defence (MoD) which had been operating a missile firing range in the northern part of South Uist for the previous forty years – but which, at that point, was planning a big reduction in range staffing. 'The cut-backs at the range got a number of us talking about how we might set about growing our economy and making ourselves less reliant on outside agencies like the MoD,' Angus MacMillan recalls. 'But no matter what we came up with by way of potential developments, we hit the same snags. We just didn't have the capital needed to lever in the finance it would take to get any really worthwhile ventures off the ground. And it was hard to see how this was going to change as long as all our resources – land, fresh water, access to the sea – were in possession of people who didn't live here and had no real stake in the place.'

The people in question were South Uist's owners. They consisted of seven families, from Lowland Scotland and further afield, who bought the property in 1960 and who then vested its ownership in a company, South Uist Estate Ltd, controlled entirely by themselves. This company's directors, known collectively in South Uist as 'the syndicate', held title to some 93,000 acres – made up of South Uist, much of the neighbouring island of Benbecula (to the north) and a scattering of smaller islands, the largest of which (off South Uist's southern coast) was Eriskay. By its owners – some of whom, by the 1990s, were resident overseas – the South Uist Estate was valued primarily for the superb angling to be got there. 'In some ways we were lucky to have landlords like the syndicate,' Angus MacMillan comments. 'They didn't cause problems of the sort other landlords caused in places like Eigg and Knoydart. All they cared about was their fishing. But that of course was why we were never going to get anywhere developmentally as long as the syndicate remained in charge. There was absolutely no reason for our landlords to set up new businesses or do anything else of great consequence. What they wanted, you might say, was to keep things much as they had always been. A lot of us, on the other hand, wanted the very opposite of that. We wanted to make changes. But to make these changes we had somehow to get control of the estate.'

Angus MacMillan, the island businessman who chairs Stòras Uibhist.

The fishery of South Uist, including sea trout, salmon and brown trout, is of international renown, and is the estate's most valuable asset in capital terms.

Bidwells, **South Uist Community Steering Group: Feasibility Study into Potential Estate Purchase,** *September 2004.*

By the opening years of the twenty-first century, the possibility of its permanent residents having some say in the management of the South Uist Estate was beginning to be explored in the course of occasional contacts involving Angus MacMillan and other local people on one side, representatives of the estate's owners on the other. But what turned these contacts into serious negotiations about a possible community buy-out, Angus MacMillan stresses, was the fact that the Scottish government's Land Reform Bill was then being taken through the Scottish parliament. 'That was absolutely fundamental,' Angus comments. 'Almost every scrap of land the syndicate owned was in crofting tenure. And the reforms that were on the way were going to make that land vulnerable to community takeover. This gave us negotiating clout we'd never have had otherwise. At last we could force the pace.'

The outcome, its widespread backing demonstrated by the result of one more of the ballots which have become a key component of the land reform process, was a negotiated purchase of South Uist Estate Ltd by Stòras Uibhist – its Gaelic designation conveying the newly formed trust's intention of enabling the community it serves to access something of the wealth bound up in natural assets which, in December 2006, were brought into this community's ownership.

Stòras Uibhist's headquarters.

The price paid for South Uist Estate Ltd and various associated companies was £4.5 million. The Scottish Land Fund – its original funding from the national lottery, and the further £5 million made available to the SLF from the same source, having been disbursed completely – was no more by 2006. But a grant equivalent to half the South Uist Estate's purchase price was awarded to Stòras Uibhist by the national lottery's Growing Community Assets programme, to which the SLF's responsibilities had been transferred. Further substantial assistance was forthcoming from various other quarters – principally HIE.

With 93,000 acres to manage and with some 3,000 estate residents to answer to, Stòras Uibhist is much the most substantial community land trust in the Highlands and Islands. The organisation's ambitions are commensurate with its size – the sheer scale of Stòras Uibhist's commercial operations making the point that, given appropriate conditions, a community land trust can become a very major business.

Stòras Uibhist's core activity remains the management of the estate taken over at the end of 2006. This estate was run at an annual loss by its previous owners – a loss they made good by selling buildings and other assets. Although such sales have been stopped, the estate is now being operated at a modest profit. Reporting to Stòras Uibhist's annual general meeting in June 2011, the trust's auditor called this 'major turnaround in the financial performance' of the property a 'remarkable' achievement. It is all the more noteworthy because the fact of the South Uist Estate no longer being loss-making, taken in conjunction with a similar state of affairs in Knoydart, gives the lie to the longstanding contention that so-called 'sporting properties' can never be viable other than when owned by the sort of people whose wealth is such as to enable them to carry operating losses often said, by these same people, to be inescapable.

Despite Stòras Uibhist having more employees than the South Uist Estate's previous owners, revenues from activities such as angling and shooting have risen much faster than costs – with takings from loch and river fishings, as Stòras Uibhist accounts show, having more than doubled between 2007 and 2010. Providing accommodation for some of the anglers who come to South Uist to access island fishings is Grogarry

As owner of the South Uist Estate, Stòras Uibhist manages 93,000 acres … covering almost the whole of the islands of Benbecula, Eriskay and South Uist, as well as a number of other small islands… Stòras Uibhist, a vibrant and forward-looking estate, is home to over 850 tenant crofters and numerous businesses, in the aquaculture, agriculture, fishing, food processing, construction, tourism and service sectors, all located amid some of the most spectacular scenery [in] … the UK.

Stòras Uibhist website, August 2011.

A major turnaround in the financial performance of the estate has taken place since the community land buy-out. Given the current economic climate, and in comparison with the performance of many other estates, the £11,000 profit achieved by Stòras Uibhist in the year is quite remarkable.

Gareth Magee, Partner, Scott Moncrieff Chartered Accountants, Edinburgh, auditor for the Stòras Uibhist group of companies, commenting at the Stòras Uibhist agm, June 2011.

Grogarry Lodge is an exclusive Hebridean retreat providing an island experience that's hard to beat. Let on an exclusive use basis, the Lodge provides serviced accommodation for up to sixteen guests in eight bedrooms, with wildfowling, stalking, hill walking and some of the best salmon, sea trout and brown trout fishing in Europe included in the package.

Stòras Uibhist website, August 2011.

Eighteen anglers, one island, a week of sunshine, an unimaginable number of lochs … I contacted Stòras Uibhist to enquire about Grogarry Lodge … The week that suited us best was available … When we arrived at the lodge, Bella, the housekeeper, asked if we were hungry. 'I'll fix a wee something for you,' she said, and reappeared five minutes later with whole haunch of wild venison, two loaves, a slab of butter and a huge fruitcake. What a start! We ate like kings for the week on the best of local produce … The weather was dreadful [for fishing]: bright sun and … light and variable winds. [But lots of fish were taken all the same] and we agreed that our week at Grogarry would stay with us all forever … A show of hands voted overwhelmingly for rebooking.

Colin McCrory, 'Unfinished Business', Trout and Salmon, December 2010.

Left: *Seonaidh Steele, Stòras Uibhist's fisheries officer, and Lorna MacLeod, who handles fisheries bookings on the South Uist Estate – where revenues from angling and field sports have risen substantially since community ownership was achieved.* **Right:** *Grogarry Lodge is an important Stòras Uibhist asset.*

Lodge, the sort of substantial residence which, if Stòras Uibhist had followed Gigha or North Harris precedent, would have been sold or not bought in the first place – but which Angus MacMillan and his fellow directors insisted on acquiring and which they have since turned into one of the trust's money-earners.

Also bringing more and more visitors to South Uist, and thus boosting prospects for island hotels and bed-and-breakfast establishments, is Askernish Golf Course which Stòras Uibhist helped back into use. Situated on dunes and grassland just to the rear of the island's Atlantic shoreline, this long-abandoned course was laid out by one of the Victorian era's most renowned golf course designers who had been hired by an estate proprietor of the time. Advertised today as 'the most natural links course in the world', Askernish, to which improvements continue to be made, has been the means of getting the name of Stòras Uibhist into – among other improbable places – *The New Yorker.*

Assisting with the restoration of Askernish Golf Course is worthwhile. Getting the South Uist Estate into profit is, for reasons stated, still more important. But for all that Stòras Uibhist's record is impressive, what matters most about the organisation is not its performance to date – but the far-reaching nature of Stòras Uibhist undertakings that, in the summer of 2011, had just started to move out of the planning stage. These undertakings merit watching because they constitute the beginnings of a nationally

Askernish Golf Course.

I got to play a couple of rounds at Askernish in December. Even though the course is further north than Sitka, Alaska, the Gulf Stream keeps temperatures on South Uist mild through most of the winter and creates the possibility of a twelve-month golf season, at least for diehards … There was a film of frost on some of the beach grass when we began, but the sky was virtually cloudless, and I never needed the stocking cap that I had tucked in my golf bag … Donald MacInnes [the Askernish Golf Club's captain] had brought his dog, which ran ahead of us over the dunes, pausing occasionally to enlarge a rabbit hole. The fairways and greens were ungroomed, in comparison with a typical course at home, and we sometimes had to play a rut or a bare spot or a half-buried skeleton of a sheep. But roughness is part of the course's charm. The bunkers looked like real hazards, rather than like oversized hotel ashtrays, and the slanting winter light made the beach grass glow.

David Owen, 'The Ghost Course', The New Yorker, *20 April 2009.*

significant experiment in how to bring about dramatic changes for the better in a place where people have lived for generations with contracting economic prospects and with a consequent exodus of population. Stòras Uibhist aims to reverse these processes by so expanding the economy of Eriskay, South Uist and Benbecula that living standards start to rise and people, instead of moving out, move in. At the heart of this strategy are two projects – each costing around £10 million – that Stòras Uibhist, at the time of writing, is set on bringing to fruition during 2012 and 2013. These involve the construction of a wind farm adjacent to Loch Carnan, towards the northern end of the South Uist Estate, and a major expansion of harbour and other facilities at Lochboisdale, South Uist's principal port and ferry terminal.

Crofting and sporting estates have traditionally been loss-making entities, primarily due to their being operated by absentee owners for sporting and leisure activity. The community buy-out of South Uist Estate Ltd was taken forward on the basis that community ownership of the islands, with a pro-active and commercial approach to economic activity, would result in the assets of the estate being used to regenerate the local economy and reverse chronic depopulation.

Stòras Uibhist, **Loch Carnan Community Wind Farm Business Plan,** *August 2009.*

The Loch Carnan project underpins much of the rationale for the South Uist Estate community buy-out. The project will allow the community company to invest in a capital asset which will deliver a long term sustainable revenue stream for reinvestment in the local community to create jobs, provide sustainable infrastructure … and reduce out-migration. The Loch Carnan Community Wind farm project has been supported by the local community … Turnout and support at community meetings has been strong and the project received no objections at planning stage.

Stòras Uibhist website, August 2011.

HIE is backing Stòras Uibhist with £5 million of investment towards a £9.9 million project to create new marine leisure and fisheries facilities, and provided access to land for community and commercial development at Lochboisdale. The new project aims to create jobs and stimulate economic and community growth in one of [our] most fragile areas. It will open up access to land for business development and community housing, as well as creating infrastructure for the fisheries and aquaculture industries and the marine tourism market. HIE estimates the development could create over 100 full-time equivalent jobs.

'Lochboisdale Port of Entry', **HIE Review,** *Summer 2011.*

The Loch Carnan wind farm will do for Stòras Uibhist what Gigha's 'dancing ladies' have done for the Isle of Gigha Heritage Trust. It will provide a revenue stream substantial enough to allow the Stòras to engage in large-scale developmental activity. To make the sort of difference in Benbecula, South Uist and Eriskay that the Isle of Gigha Heritage Trust has made in Gigha, however, Stòras Uibhist needs to think big. Hence the project's very substantial upfront capital cost – the bulk of which is coming from a loan negotiated with a major bank.

Because the Loch Carnan wind farm is more than ten times larger than its Gigha counterpart, the wind farm's output, when sold into the national grid, will provide Stòras Uibhist with an annual income (after loan repayments) of somewhere between £600,000 and £800,000. Revenues of this sort, which should start to become available in early 2013, will give Stòras Uibhist the financial muscle the trust requires to make the most of the commercial and other opportunities opened up by its planned

Huw Francis, Stòras Uibhist's chief executive.

redevelopment of Lochboisdale. Although, at the time of writing, not quite all the cash needed to meet the £9.9 million cost of this project's first phase had been got together, prospects for it had already been boosted by HIE's decision, in the spring of 2011, to invest £5 million in the venture – and, with most of the remaining funding also secured, Angus MacMillan and his Stòras Uibhist colleagues are confident of their soon being able to tender initial construction contracts. The resulting works – including a causeway linking an offshore island to the South Uist mainland – will provide all sorts of new harbour facilities as well as space for harbour-side housing and other developments. Hence HIE's decision to become involved in an initiative which, the agency calculates, has the potential to provide South Uist with at least a hundred badly needed jobs.

Characteristically, Angus MacMillan is already looking forward to what comes next at Lochboisdale which, once all of Stòras Uibhist's planned redevelopments have taken place, will have been turned into one of the deepest-water harbours in the north-west of Scotland. It will be important, Angus says, for Lochboisdale to position itself in such a way as to make the port a lead contender to provide the facilities that will be required by companies constructing offshore wind farms – or, for that matter, drilling for oil and gas – in the Atlantic to the west of the Hebrides. It will be equally important, Angus continues, for Lochboisdale to become the means of providing South Uist with improved, and more direct, ferry sailings to the Scottish mainland. 'We might well think about taking a stake in a new ferry ourselves,' the Stòras Uibhist chairman comments.

In some quarters, both in South Uist and beyond, aspirations of this sort tend to be dismissed as unattainable, far-fetched, fanciful. The existence of such views is understandable. For reasons mentioned in connection with Gigha people's initial hesitations about taking ownership of their island, the Highlands and Islands have never run short of doubters, sceptics and pessimists. But what is so unimaginable about Stòras Uibhist investing in, perhaps even owning outright, something as basic to South Uist's future wellbeing as a fast, up-to-date ferry? The notion is certainly a lot less outlandish than it would have been to suggest in 1991 that, inside just twenty years, more than half the land in the Outer Hebrides would have been brought into community ownership.

... to the highest mountain tops. The peak in the centre, Sgurr Coire Choinneachain, is on the Knoydart Foundation's community-owned estate.

6

A story not yet ended

Benefits and costs of community land ownership
Obstacles to progress
Isle of Rum Community Trust
Pairc Trust
Reviewing the Land Reform (Scotland) Act 2003
and reinstating the Scottish Land Fund

CHAPTER SIX

A story not yet ended

Benefits and costs of community land ownership § Obstacles to progress
Isle of Rum Community Trust § Pairc Trust
Reviewing the Land Reform (Scotland) Act 2003 and reinstating the
Scottish Land Fund

In December 1992, shortly after members of the Assynt Crofters Trust bought the North Lochinver Estate, Allan MacRae, the trust's chairman, was asked by a journalist if he and other crofters were up to the task of managing a landed property of the sort that had always previously been owned and run by people of great wealth. Could crofters really do better by Assynt than its private landlords had done? 'Well,' Allan said, 'I can't see how we can do any worse.'

The same answer could have been given to much the same question in many of the places featured in this book. In fairness, across the Highlands and Islands private landownership's more recent record contains nothing on a par with what was done by earlier lairds. With the exception of Eigg and Gigha, where evictions seemed imminent during the 1990s, none of the localities dealt with in this book experienced in the twentieth century anything approaching the insecurity that was practically universal when the owners of estate after estate were turning family after family – Allan MacRae's forebears among them – out of their homes. Crofting protest and the resulting intervention of the state long ago brought an end to oppression and exploitation of that type. But other than when a Runciman, a Horlick or some similarly generous individual invested in a particular property, there was seldom much sign of twentieth-century lairds engaging seriously – certainly not for lengthy periods – with the developmental requirements of the estates now in community ownership. Suppose such ownership had not taken off in the Highlands and Islands in the way it did after the breakthrough achieved by Allan MacRae and his colleagues in Assynt. Suppose, as would then have been the case, that Stòras Uibhist or the Isle of Gigha Heritage Trust had never existed. Is it conceivable, in these circumstances,

Rum viewed from Eigg. Cleared almost totally in 1826 when some 300 of its people were evicted, Rum is beginning to be acquired by its present-day residents.

that any private landlord would be getting together the finance required to regenerate the Lochboisdale harbour area in order to create a hundred or more jobs? Is it likely, in these same circumstances, that some other laird would be supervising, and spending heavily on, the refurbishment of Gigha's entire housing stock? The evidence suggests that it is not.

But if it would have been hard for community-controlled land trusts to do less well than private landlords of the sort who made such a mess of many of the places now in community ownership, neither was it anticipated, even by community ownership's most impassioned advocates, that such organisations would turn out to be as effective as they have been. Something of what has been achieved by community ownership trusts is apparent from preceding chapters. The positive story they tell is reinforced by growing numbers of independent assessments and academic analyses of what these

Willie McSporran of the Isle of Gigha Heritage Trust with one of the trust's wind turbines – part of Britain's first community-owned and grid-connected windfarm.

trusts have done and are doing – by way of expanding local economies, assisting the emergence of new businesses, boosting living standards, adding to population and ensuring that financial returns from renewable energy projects remain in the localities where these projects are situated.

Our research shows that community land ownership is playing a successful role in strengthening rural Scotland's communities. It is leading to the 're-peopling' of rural Scotland by enabling existing residents to remain in remote areas and encouraging in-migration. This is because ownership is giving communities the opportunity to increase local employment and develop revenue streams through the creation of new business, the building of affordable housing, the sustaining of rural schools and the delivery of basic infrastructure such as roads and electricity … Community land ownership is one clear way of achieving a more vibrant rural Scotland.

Sarah Skerratt, Senior Researcher and Team Leader, Rural Society Research, Scottish Agricultural College, July 2011.

My experience over many years is that if you give people … ownership of land then you get real benefits. You just have to look at Eigg and Gigha to see how community ownership works, with increased population, especially of young people, increased business opportunities and greater community confidence.

Michael Foxley, Leader of Administration, Highland Council, speaking at a council conference on land reform, 23 March 2010.

There is something intrinsically right about [a] local community owning [its] own land … Ownership unleashes new ideas, new projects, new entrepreneurship, new community confidence.

Angus Campbell, Vice-Convener, Comhairle nan Eilean Siar, January 2007: West Highland Free Press, 19 January 2007.

A recurring theme which emerges strongly from the early years of community ownership is that the quantifiable benefits, important as they are, are outshone by a web of intangible but valuable outcomes … These include improved social cohesion and confidence, transformations in community pride and spirit, and optimism about the future – a future in which local people now have a personal stake.

Charles Warren, Managing Scotland's Environment, Edinburgh University Press, 2009.

Most of this is quantifiable – and is beginning to be quantified. More difficult to measure, but arguably of still greater significance, is the manner in which individuals involved in community ownership gain in self-esteem and self-confidence – attributes which, in turn, underpin their demonstrable capacity to take on tasks they would formerly have thought beyond them. Simply to talk with the people who manage community land trusts, or to sit in on one of their regular meetings, is to see and hear this new and impressive assurance coming through over and over again.

Community ownership as it has taken shape in the Highlands and Islands, then, is a Scottish success story. This makes it puzzling – especially to community land trusts themselves – that the community ownership movement has attracted of late so little attention from Scotland's more prominent politicians.

Their apparent lack of interest may be bound up with something mentioned in this book's opening chapter – a longstanding tendency on the part of some sections of the Scottish press to misunderstand or misrepresent the community ownership movement. Despite community land trusts consisting overwhelmingly of 'ordinary people' (in the standard media phrase) who are working hard, taking control of their lives, standing on their own feet and otherwise following the advice that newspapers and commentators habitually hand out to society at large, these same newspapers and commentators are firmly of the view that ownership of the Highlands and Islands by anyone other than lairds of the traditional variety is something that ought automatically to be suspected, deplored and resisted – on the grounds, it seems, that land reform is some sort of leftist conspiracy intended to result in huge sums of public money being spent to absolutely no effect.

In fact, land reform's positive outcomes, as already stressed, are obvious – and its costs, relatively speaking, are minimal. Take, for example, the case of Eigg – its residents, for no very apparent cause, attracting particular ire in certain media quarters. Of the £1.5 million it took to put the Isle of Eigg Heritage Trust – as opposed to Marlin Eckhart aka Maruma – in charge of Eigg, only £17,000, or barely one per cent of the total, came from taxpayers. Public money, together with grant aid from national lottery sources, has of course played a greater part in most subsequent land trust purchases. But in the context of overall national expenditure the amounts involved remain extremely small.

Over the period between 1992 and 2010, HIE made £9,484,050 available to assist with the land purchase costs of community ownership trusts in the Highlands and Islands. Between 2001 and 2010, trusts obtained a further £15,910,067 for the same purpose from national lottery sources: from the Scottish Land Fund between 2001 and 2006; from the lottery's Growing Community Assets programme after 2006. Since lottery funding, strictly speaking, is not public money, because it is not derived from taxation, it should not really be included in any calculation of the public expenditure outlays involved in community ownership initiatives. But if it is so included, and if allowance is made for occasional contributions from non-HIE public bodies such as Scottish Natural Heritage and local authorities, the total public expenditure contribution (both tax-funded and lottery-funded) to the cost of buying land in the Highlands and Islands in order to get this land into community ownership has been in the order of £26 million.

Community ownership trusts have also accessed funding – from HIE, the national lottery, European Union and various other sources – to help with post-purchase costs of one kind or another. Where funding has gone into ventures such as constructing a wind turbine or a new building, this funding has generally been provided to land trusts on much the same basis as assistance of the same sort would be made available to other applicants for it. While developmental activity of the type thus financed is a consequence of community ownership, and indeed one of the key reasons why such ownership makes sense in public policy terms, it is not, then, a cost of such ownership – and should not be so regarded.

More difficulty to compute is the cash aid – from HIE and lottery sources – extended to community ownership trusts to help with costs such as those involved in trusts providing themselves with office premises or employing development officers and other staff. When trusts have been getting up and running, such costs have usually been met largely by HIE, the national lottery or both. Because of the difficulty of disaggregating expenditure in this area from other related expenditure, it has proved impossible to put a precise figure on it. But spending of this type is calculated here – though this is probably an overestimate – to be in the region of £4 million.

On this basis, overall assistance – from the national lottery and the public purse – to the community land sector in the Highlands and Islands can be put at around £30 million over nearly twenty years. This is no negligible sum. But it is no more than the cost of each 600-yard stretch of the tramway that will one day link Edinburgh's airport with the city centre. It is about one-fifteenth of the bill for a five-mile stretch of motorway completed in Glasgow in 2011. And it is equivalent to what farmers and landowners get by way of agricultural support, or subsidy, in the United Kingdom every three or four days.

David Cameron, chairman of Community Land Scotland, with some of the many new homes built as a result of community ownership initiatives.

[A] major theme that was articulated by many community land trusts is a requirement for recognition that community land trusts do deliver. There is evidence of businesses created ... services being delivered that were formerly implemented by local authorities ... spin-offs from investment including jobs, housing, green energy [and] recycling ... revenue-generating projects which save government money ... Community land trusts would welcome systematic visits from Edinburgh to communities to see evidence [of this] on the ground.

Sarah Skerratt, Community Land Ownership and Community Resilience: Rural Policy Centre Research Report, Scottish Agricultural College, June 2011.

This is not to suggest that Edinburgh should not have trams, that Glasgow should not have motorways or that farmers and landowners should not receive subsidies. It is to contend, however, that community ownership's price-tag is by no means excessive and that, given the good things thus achieved, expenditure on the community land sector is at least as justifiable, on any cost-benefit basis, as other forms of state spending. There is, then, no reason – certainly no reason deriving from the financial outlays land reform has involved – for any First Minister of Scotland to shy away from direct engagement with the community land trusts now transforming so many parts of the Highlands and Islands. But there has been little such engagement on the part of the four men who have held the office of First Minister since 1999. Labour's Jack McConnell, so far the longest serving of the four, visited Assynt in 2002. But there have been no subsequent such visits to places like Eigg, Knoydart, Gigha or South Uist – certainly no recent first ministerial equivalent of the trip Prime Minister David Cameron made in August 2011 to Cumbria's Eden District where he saw at first hand something of the achievements of one of England's community land trusts.

This is not to imply that any of Scotland's First Ministers, Donald Dewar (Labour), Henry McLeish (Labour), Jack McConnell (Labour) and Alex Salmond (SNP), have been or are hostile to land reform. In fact, all have been supportive of it. But it nevertheless regrettable that, up to the time of writing in September 2011, despite some such engagement on the part of other Scottish Ministers, there has been no recent First Ministerial meeting of a high-profile and well-reported type with community ownership activists in one or other of the places where these activists live. This matters because, as Allan MacRae remarked when he met with the then Secretary of State for Scotland, Michael Forsyth, in the course of the latter's 1995 trip to Assynt, people trying to make things better at a local level are encouraged when their country's leading figures take a personal interest in what they are about. And it matters for the more important reason that if Alex Salmond, the present First Minister, were to do as Michael Forsyth did, people at the community ownership front line would be given a chance to explain to the man in charge of Scotland's government just what is needed by way of policy initiatives if the community land sector is to grow further.

Although there are others, three such initiatives are particularly required. They concern the interlocking issues of how to finance community land buy-outs, how to ensure that land in public ownership can be transferred more cheaply to community ownership trusts and how to remedy the increasingly apparent failings of the Land Reform (Scotland) Act of 2003.

———————

When it was decided that the Scottish Land Fund should cease to exist in 2006 as a distinct national lottery programme and that its responsibilities should be transferred to another such programme, Growing Community Assets (GCA), this did not result, as Stòras Uibhist experience shows, in land trusts losing all access to funding of the SLF type. But it meant that there was no longer any pot of money earmarked for their exclusive use – bids for assistance with land acquisition now being in competition with innumerable other, equally valid, claims on GCA resources. Making this situation still more dispiriting from the community land movement's perspective was the fact of its having coincided with a period when the budget available to Highlands and Islands Enterprise was being reduced sharply by Scotland's government. While some part of this cut-back in HIE funding was indubitably due to wider pressures on Scottish government finances, and while HIE, the national lottery and Scottish ministers would doubtless insist that the funding position is by no means as bleak as the community land sector's representatives believe it to be, the cumulative effect of the SLF's loss and funding cuts at HIE has been to create a pervasive impression in today's Highlands and Islands that neither the purchase of a piece of land by a community, nor the post-purchase developments which give point to such an acquisition, will be as well supported today as they were formerly.

The community ownership movement's consequent sense of having had funding difficulties placed in its way has been reinforced by the national lottery's increasing, and understandable, reluctance to help communities buy land in the possession of agencies like HIE, the Forestry Commission and the Scottish government's agricultural department. Cash raised by the lottery, its administrators insist, cannot and must not take the place of tax-funded public expenditure. But that is exactly what happens if, for example, a community group receives several hundred thousand pounds from the Growing Community Assets programme and then uses this money to buy a tract of woodland from Forestry Commission Scotland – thereby reducing the calls FCS would otherwise make on the taxpayer. The obvious way around this difficulty would be a return to principles enunciated by Michael Forsyth in connection with his Transfer of Crofting Estates Act of 1997 – legislation which, according to the then Secretary of State, was intended to enable him and his successors to make state-owned croft land available to community trusts at low or zero prices. The post-1997 abandonment of this approach, and the related insistence that land belonging to government or its agencies can only be disposed of at market price, have together had the effect, as indicated already, of delaying West Harris's move into community ownership and of making any such move at Orbost quite impossible. In other places, meanwhile, community interest in Forestry Commission landholdings in particular is being stifled – rural residents

Fresh water, land and ocean in the Hebrides.

seeing little point in embarking on purchase projects they suspect will founder on their inability to raise the necessary finance.

Reducing the cost to communities of taking over land in public ownership requires action by the UK government. This is apparent from Clause 1(4) of the Transfer of Crofting Estates Act. That clause reads: 'The disposal of property under this Act shall be on such terms as the Secretary of State, *with the consent of the Treasury*, may agree with the body acquiring the property.' Although authority to give effect to any such disposal rests today with the Scottish government, not the Secretary of State for Scotland, the import of the 1997 Act's provisions, including the six words italicised here, remain as before. These six words constitute the stumbling block encountered in West Harris – the consent needed for a cost-free handover of that locality's government-owned crofting estates to the people living on them not being forthcoming. And for all that the Transfer of Crofting Estates Act had no role in the planned establishment of community ownership at Orbost, the obstacle met with there was identical. Orbost residents, HIE was told by the Scottish government ministers and civil servants to whom the agency is ultimately responsible, could not take control of the HIE-owned land on which they live without paying a market price for it. Might the Conservative-Liberal Democrat coalition in power at Westminster since May 2010 be persuaded – whether by Scotland's devolved administration, by Community Land Scotland or others – to relax this restrictive stance? Such relaxation would certainly be in accord with Prime Minister David Cameron's commitment to a state which, in pursuit of 'opportunities for people to take control of their lives', ought to be 'galvanising, catalysing, prompting, encouraging and agitating for community engagement'. So far, however, there has been no hint of any significant modification of UK Treasury thinking in this area.

For much of the Westminster coalition's time in office, as it happens, a Liberal Democrat MP from a Highlands and Islands constituency, Danny Alexander, has been Chief Secretary to the Treasury – a key ministerial portfolio in this context. Alexander is supportive of the community land sector. He made this clear in July 2011 when launching a UK-wide Coastal Communities Fund consisting of half of the revenues

We need a thoughtful re-imagination of the role, as well as the size, of the state … The re-imagined state should not stop at creating opportunities for people to take control of their lives. It must actively help people take advantage of this new freedom. This means a new role for the state: actively helping to create the Big Society … galvanising, catalysing, prompting, encouraging and agitating for community engagement and social renewal.

David Cameron, then Leader of the Opposition, Hugo Young Memorial Lecture, 10 November 2009.

accruing to the Crown Estate Commission (the body in control of Britain's seabed) from port authorities, fish farmers, offshore wind farm developers and the various other interests obliged by the commission to make regular payments in order to obtain access to the marine resources they require. The Highlands and Islands share of this new fund, Danny Alexander said, will amount initially to some £2 million annually – some proportion of which, the chief secretary indicated, might be used 'to boost community land ownership'.

All such gestures are positive and Danny Alexander's was greeted as such by Community Land Scotland. An easing of Treasury rules on public land disposals to communities would have been even more appreciated by CLS, however. Such an easing, the organisation stresses, will remain high on its agenda. But if Community Land Scotland – moving on purposefully from its Harris conference of March 2011 – is committed to lobbying the UK coalition on the land disposals issue, CLS is equally intent, indeed rather more intent, on making the community land sector case as strongly as possible to Scotland's SNP government.

This government began as a minority administration in 2007. Since the election of May 2011, however, it has had an overall majority in the Scottish Parliament.

The [British] government will establish a UK-wide Coastal Communities Fund to support economic development in coastal communities. The fund, which will be open for business from April 2012, will be worth 50 per cent of the gross revenues from the Crown Estate's marine activities … On the basis of 2010–11 revenues, that would entail almost £2 million for the Highlands and Islands … The fund will be open to a wide range of organisations … In the Highlands and Islands I particularly encourage bids that seek to boost community land ownership across the area – given the track record of economic development that this brings.

Danny Alexander, Chief Secretary to the Treasury, speaking in Stornoway, 21 July 2011.

Community land trusts identified the importance of Community Land Scotland as an organisation to lobby on their behalf … There was felt to be great value in having a single body representing a collective of community land owners.

Sarah Skerratt, Community Land Ownership and Community Resilience: Rural Policy Centre Research Report, Scottish Agricultural College, June 2011.

Community Land Scotland's purposes are:
§ Representation of community landowners to all levels of government, to educational institutions and to funding organisations;
§ Information and skills exchange between members;
§ To work long-term with like-minded organisations;
§ To become self-financing and have funds available for community land purchase and development.

Statement of Community Land Scotland objectives, September 2011.

Among the MSPs constituting that majority, and among SNP government ministers, are people who were active in the Scottish National Party when, towards the end of their 1973 tour of the Highlands and Islands, John McGrath and his 7:84 Theatre Company got a telephone call from William Wolfe, then the SNP's leader. Would they be prepared, Wolfe asked McGrath and his colleagues, to mount a performance of *The Cheviot, the Stag and the Black, Black Oil* at that year's annual conference of the Scottish National Party? Thus it came about that conference delegates heard John McGrath's powerful call for land reform – a call to which those same delegates responded by giving McGrath and his cast a ten-minute-long standing ovation. The SNP which thus applauded *The Cheviot, the Stag and the Black, Black Oil* was a party far from power. Today this same party is in a position to do what, that night in 1973, its conference delegates indubitably wanted done. Being in sole charge of Scotland's government, First Minister Alex Salmond and his ministerial team could readily give both backing and leadership to Highlands and Islands communities where community ownership has been achieved – as well as to those other communities where such ownership has still to be accomplished.

This might be all the more appropriate because of its being possible to discern in the community ownership movement's successes something akin to the rejuvenating effect the SNP asserts would be produced more widely by Scotland gaining independence. Just such a connection was made by Ian Scarr-Hall, the North Harris Trust's close partner, when this English businessman took up a pro-SNP position. His witnessing at first hand in Harris the 'immeasurable energy released when a community takes ownership of [its] destiny,' Ian Scarr-Hall wrote in 2010, had led him 'to believe in freedom and independence for Scotland'.

One indication that the SNP might be prepared to tackle funding and other difficulties in the way of further community ownership is provided by events in Rum – an island adjacent to Eigg and one that has belonged for more than half a century to Scottish Natural Heritage (SNH) or to this conservation agency's predecessor bodies. Since Rum's clearance in 1826 – when several hundred islanders were evicted and shipped to Nova Scotia – the island's population has been small.

Some years ago, I worked with the people of North Harris to help deliver what was at the time the largest community buy-out in Scotland … Being a partner with the community … enabled me to witness the immeasurable energy that is released when a community takes ownership of [its] destiny. Whisky, oil and many other material products are valuable assets, but these are minor when compared to the value of energy released when people are given freedom to govern their own future. There was something indescribably empowering [about] standing with a group of people and charting a new, brighter future. And that is the same sentiment that has led me to believe in independence and freedom for Scotland.

Ian Scarr-Hall, 'Full independence would benefit both Scotland and England', Scotsman, 14 January 2010.

Lesley Watt along with her partner Neil Boyd are set to become [in the summer of 2011] the first crofters on the Isle of Rum in the modern era. The whole of the island was previously owned and managed as a National Nature Reserve by Scottish Natural Heritage. However, assets and land … were transferred [recently] … into the ownership of the Isle of Rum Community Trust (IRCT) and three … crofts were created. The IRCT objectives for the crofts are to provide security of tenure on the island, to encourage both local and new people to take up crofting activities and to encourage a sustainable economic base for the Isle of Rum community.

Isle of Rum Community website, August 2011.

Nor was there much prospect of this situation changing as long as SNH retained total control. Because most islanders were employed by SNH, and because island homes and other facilities were owned by SNH, the Rum community could neither grow nor attain much, if anything, by way of autonomy. Hence the growing demand from islanders for some part of the island to go into community ownership – a demand that promptly ran up against the standard difficulty that any disposal of government-owned assets (including Rum and everything on it) should go ahead only on the basis that the new owners of those assets pay the going market rate for them. Fortunately for Rum residents, the Scottish government minister responsible for environmental matters, and thus for Scottish Natural Heritage, at the start of the SNP's first term of office in 2007 was determined that, by one means or another, he was going to get a strategically crucial slice of Rum into community ownership. The minister in question was Michael Russell. His refusal to be obstructed by the market value roadblock resulted in the Isle of Rum Community Trust (IRCT), which islanders had set up to progress community ownership, being – in effect – given a grant by SNH of some £230,000 so that the trust could then buy from SNH a total of 360 acres in and around Kinloch, the island's only settlement. Today, as a result, all sorts of projects are being taken forward. One such project involves the creation of a number of crofts on land now in IRCT ownership. These began to be allocated to prospective occupants in the summer of 2011 which means that, for the first time since the island's clearance nearly 200 years ago, there are today crofters living on Rum.

Had HIE been encouraged and permitted – which it was not – to do at Orbost what SNH was thus allowed to do in Rum, Orbost would now be in community ownership. Were similar arrangements available to crofters on the Keoldale Estate in Sutherland, owned by the Scottish government's Rural and Environment Directorate, the successor body to DAFS, then Keoldale, where there continues to be interest in taking over the property, would doubtless be in community ownership as well. For the moment, however, Rum is a one-off. It is likely to remain so until the SNP government as a whole (as opposed to individual ministers) gives a higher priority than it has given so far to getting state-owned land into community control.

But fixing this problem ought ideally to be just one component of a wider land reform agenda. Prominent among other components should be a streamlined and simplified version of the Land Reform Act of 2003. The need for this has been comprehensively demonstrated by developments on the Pairc Estate in the Lochs district of Lewis.

People living on this estate began to plan a community purchase of the property just prior to the 2003 Act taking effect. The estate, in the south-eastern corner of Lewis, is 26,800 acres in extent and some 400 people live within its boundaries. As was the case on the Galson Estate, where community ownership started to be thought about at much the same time, Pairc in 2003 was the possible site of a big wind farm – the potential developer in Pairc being Scottish and Southern Energy. Also like Galson and, for that matter, South Uist, another area where buy-out proposals were being progressed in 2003, the Pairc Estate is almost all in crofting tenure. Pairc residents, therefore, are very much the sort of folk meant to benefit from Part Three of the Land Reform Act – this being the section of the Act which entitles a crofting community to take ownership of the croft land in its neighbourhood. When they first attempted to exercise that crofting community right-to-buy, Pairc people were not alone in so doing – groups in South Uist and Galson, as mentioned in the preceding chapter, having then been contemplating much the same course. In Galson and South Uist, however, the landlords thus targeted eventually reached negotiated understandings with Urras Oighreachd Ghabhsainn in the one case and with Stòras Uibhist in the other. This did not happen in Pairc where the relevant landowner, Barry Lomas, a Leamington Spa accountant, was from the outset – and is still today – intent on contesting the purchase of his estate by the Pairc Trust, the locally constituted organisation looking to bring Pairc into community ownership.

Had the Land Reform Act's provisions produced the results that the Scottish parliament intended them to produce in 2003, no crofting landlord would have been able to fend off community ownership in the way that such ownership has been fended off in Pairc. But both in Pairc and more widely, the task of bringing land into community ownership has not been helped nearly as much as is sometimes imagined by an Act which, for all that it was thought originally to be of huge significance, has failed for the most part to deliver what was expected of it. Although the circumstances surrounding the 2003 legislation's adoption were such as to send out a powerful signal to the effect that an overwhelming majority of Scotland's parliamentarians backed community ownership of land, neither the Act's Part Two (giving all Scottish rural communities some chance of becoming involved in such ownership) nor its Part Three (dealing with crofting localities) have been of much practical use. Most of the community purchases described in this book either predated the Land Reform Act or took place without recourse to it. And when, in Pairc, a community trust did resort to the Act in order to buy croft land from a crofting landlord who did not want to sell it, the trust was soon bogged down in legal requirements of almost unbelievable complexity.

This complexity is nowhere more evident than in the nature of the maps which the Land Reform Act obliges an 'applicant body' like the Pairc Trust to compile. These maps, as well as delineating the boundaries of the property in which applicants are interested, have to contain immense amounts of detail. They must show, for example, all the 'sewers, pipes, lines, watercourses or other conduits' to be found on a tract of usually hilly terrain extending to many thousands of acres; they must show 'fences, dykes, ditches or other boundaries'; and, as if that were not bad enough, they must be accompanied by proof that the applicant body supplying them has made 'reasonably diligent enquiry' (a most slippery phrase) to 'ascertain' the existence of any features it might somehow have missed. Mapping to this standard is not required of the parties to any other property transaction that takes place in the United Kingdom. Indeed the level of accuracy demanded may well be unattainable – in that it could take almost forever to be sure one had found, for example, every 'watercourse or conduit' on a rain-drenched Hebridean hillside. Little wonder, then, that Simon Fraser, a lawyer with unrivalled experience of these matters, has told the author that to map a piece of croft land in strict compliance with the Land Reform Act would cost more than this land is worth.

There are people in the community land movement who wonder about the reasons for this state of affairs. Giving *every* crofting community the right-to-buy given in 1997 to crofting communities on state-owned land, these people point out, was one of the key recommendations made by the Land Reform Policy Group in 1998 and 1999. Included in early versions of the then Scottish Executive's Land Reform Bill, this crofting community right-to-buy was afterwards dropped – partly as a result of lobbying from landowning interests and partly because senior civil servants felt a change in the law affecting crofters should wait for a Crofting Bill and should not be tacked on, or so civil servants argued, to a measure with much wider implications. The consequent disappearance from the Land Reform Bill of much the most radical aspect of the programme devised by the Land Reform Policy Group resulted in heavyweight political pressure being brought to bear on the executive from inside the pro-reform camp. It was consequently agreed that the Bill should, after all, include provisions entitling all crofting communities to purchase, at a time of their choosing, croft land in their vicinity – those provisions now constituting Part Three of the Land Reform Act. Given the extent to which Part Three enables communities to challenge established property rights, it is unsurprising that it should have been drafted in such a way as to ensure that no such challenge could be mounted without considerable effort on the part of the community making it. But given the controversy surrounding this aspect of the legislation, and in particular the fact of its being dropped entirely from one version of the Bill, it is equally unsurprising that some community ownership activists believe it is not wholly accidental that the Act's mapping and other requirements are such as to have made the measure's Part Three – the part restored to the Act under protest – more or less inoperable.

Angus McDowall (left) and John Randall of the Pairc Trust.

Be that as it may, it is certainly the case that, when the Pairc Trust (having already encountered all sorts of difficulties) applied (in accordance with Land Reform Act prescriptions) for the ministerial order needed if their purchase was to go forward in the face of proprietorial opposition, the trust encountered delay after delay. The order, which could have been issued by the relevant SNP minister, Roseanna Cunningham, in October 2010, and which trust members were told they would definitely have by December, was not in the end forthcoming until the following March. From the Pairc Trust's perspective, this looked like inexcusable shilly-shallying on the minister's part. A more charitable explanation can be sought in the high probability that Roseanna

We have been trying to buy our estate for the community since 2004 and have faced obstacle after obstacle, first from the landlord, and now it seems from the Scottish government. Frustration has long since turned to anger. Twice ministers have told us a decision is imminent and twice the deadlines have come and gone with absolutely no explanation. We feel we are just being hung out to dry … Our community continues to stagnate and is prevented from sharing in the benefits of community ownership which we see all around us. The landlord of Scalpay is offering his estate free to the local people because he recognises the benefits of community ownership … Other areas, such as South Uist, Galson, Eigg, and Gigha, are forging ahead with projects to create local jobs and reverse population decline … It has been within ministers' power to decide our applications since last October. We have overwhelming public support for our cause, which is fully in line with the intentions of the legislation. The whole community would now like a decision. If the legislation is unworkable, perhaps we could just be told this, and be put out of our misery.

Angus McDowall, Chairman, Pairc Trust, March 2011: Pairc Trust press release, 8 March 2011.

Cunningham (whom Conservative MSP Bill Aitken had accused in 2003 of wanting 'more extreme' land reform than the then Scottish Executive) was by no means averse to doing as the Pairc Trust requested – but was proceeding cautiously in order to mitigate the risk of a ministerial order being challengeable in the courts.

Given these difficulties, it is much to be welcomed that the manifesto on which the SNP fought and won the Scottish election of 2011 contained a commitment to review the workings of the Land Reform Act. It is still more to be welcomed that the SNP manifesto also pledged the party to 'establish a new Scottish Land Fund'.

Speaking in July 2006, at the last meeting of the original land fund's governing committee, David Campbell, who had chaired the fund since its inception, commented that, 'when the history of land reform in Scotland came to be written', the SLF and the people who managed it, would 'deserve some recognition'. He was right. Of all the externally-sourced financial help with acquisition costs that has reached community ownership trusts in the Highlands and Islands since 1992, something like 40 per cent came in just five years from the Scottish Land Fund. While the SLF's demise, to repeat a previous point, did not result in the community land movement losing access to lottery funding, no other national lottery programme shared or shares the objective the Scottish Land Fund was given in order to make clear that it was in business primarily to promote land reform – this objective being to 'diversify the pattern of land ownership in Scotland'. An application for SLF assistance, in other words, could major on the fact of the applicant group wishing simply to establish community ownership of a piece of land in a way that an application to another lottery programme cannot – applicant groups today having to demonstrate, in a way that is necessarily tentative in advance of community ownership actually being achieved, what will result in the way of development from a community purchase. It is understandable, therefore, that the SLF continues to be missed. Hence the inclusion of this sentence in a Scottish Agricultural College research report of July 2011: 'There is consensus from all community land trusts that the Scottish Land Fund must be reinstated.' As the same report noted, land reform legislation, however revised and perfected, can do no more than create a *right* to take land into community

A ceilidh dance in Uist.

One of the success factors of the SLF has been its delivery. The SLF generated a real enthusiasm among all of those involved in it … It is doubtful that the same positive impacts could have been achieved without this level of commitment and support.

SQW Consultants, **Scottish Land Fund Evaluation: Final Report,** *May 2007.*

ownership. If this right is to be exercised, then the financial *means* of doing so have to be available. Much the best way of providing those means would be to re-establish the Scottish Land Fund.

This is what Community Land Scotland want, and this is what the Scottish National Party's recent election manifesto promised will be done – the manifesto also pledging that 'proposals in this area' would be in place 'by the end of 2011'. At the time of writing, it is impossible to know what will happen next. But given that Richard Lochhead, the Scottish government's Rural Affairs and Environment Minister, has said that he and his colleagues want to encourage and promote the expansion of community ownership of land and given that the Scottish Spending Review of September 2011 included a commitment to establish a new land fund, there is cause to hope that the story this book tells is a story not yet ended.

We believe it is time for a review of Scotland's land reform legislation … We will establish a Land Reform Review Group to advise on this … We will also establish a new Scottish Land Fund and will set out our proposals in this area by the end of 2011.

SNP Manifesto, April 2011.

We think it's important to re-establish the [Scottish] Land Fund and we've given a commitment to do that … We want to encourage land buy-outs … It's very important for rural communities to have the opportunity to take control of their land where that is possible.

Richard Lochhead, the Scottish government's Rural Affairs and Environment Minister, speaking on BBC TV during the Scottish election campaign of 2011.

The SNP manifesto for the Scottish election this year committed the SNP to reviewing current land reform legislation with a view to improving it … Two of the buy-outs I have been involved with illustrate, in different ways, the weaknesses with current legislation. In Pairc, the [trust] has faced the enormous task of mapping an estate … In West Harris, the community faced other legal obstacles because the land was government-owned. Processes like this need to be simplified … We are also committed to establishing a new Scottish Land Fund … Fragile communities need to be able to develop and to take charge of their own destiny … but to do this they need reliable sources of funding.

Alasdair Allan MSP, (SNP: Western Isles), news release, 8 July 2011.

Perspective

In October 1991, as mentioned in a previous chapter, Alastair McIntosh, one of the founders of what was then called the Isle of Eigg Trust, spoke at a public meeting on Eigg. He asked his audience to think about a future wholly different both from Eigg's past and from what was then the island's present. In this time to come, Alastair said, if a visitor to Eigg were to ask local children who owned the island, they would not name some faraway aristocrat, banker, property developer, heiress, rock star or sheikh. They would say simply, 'Us.'

In the autumn of 1991 the possibility of community ownership being established on government-owned estates in Skye and Raasay had come to nothing, and the Assynt Crofters Trust would not take shape until the following summer. In these circumstances, it was understandable that Eigg's then landlord regarded Alastair McIntosh's hopes for the island as not so much a vision, more a fantasy. Nor was he alone. Given the difficulties Eigg residents faced in the early 1990s, there could have been few, if any, of Alastair's listeners at that public meeting who were unshakeably confident that Eigg would ever be as Alastair asked them to imagine it.

But what was once hard to envisage has now come to pass. And not only on Eigg. Today you can stand on any one of more than 500,000 acres in widely separated parts of the Highlands and Islands and, on asking some local person who owns that acre, get the answer Alastair McIntosh said twenty years ago might one day be given on Eigg, 'Us.'

This represents a magnificent achievement on the part of many people. These people – the organisers, members and supporters of a whole set of community ownership trusts – have changed fundamentally and irrevocably a land ownership pattern that, prior to Assynt crofters' victory in December 1992, often seemed beyond altering. In the process, community trusts have unleashed all sorts of entrepreneurial and other energies. They have established that depopulation can be reversed, businesses created and homes built in localities where these things formerly seemed impossible;

they have demonstrated that wind power and other resources can be harnessed for local purposes; they have proved that previously loss-making estates can be run at a profit; they have shown, by embarking on native woodland regeneration and by undertaking lots of other such initiatives, that people living in the Highlands and Islands are just as capable as any outside body of sustaining and enhancing the area's outstanding natural environment.

Nothing of this has been easy. As those most involved with it are quick to tell you, establishing community ownership is one thing, making it work quite another. Enormous amounts of unpaid effort – accompanied sometimes by argument, dispute and division – have been expended in order to deliver the positive outcomes this book describes.

Maintaining such commitment is a constant challenge. That is why it is by no means impossible that, sooner or later, one – or more than one – of the local land trusts operating in the Highlands and Islands will get into financial difficulty, maybe even go under. If or when this happens, critics and opponents of community ownership will insist that the community ownership concept has thereby been invalidated. They will be wrong. The bankruptcy of a conventionally structured company – something which happens every day – does not of itself indicate that other companies are bound to meet the same fate. Nor will the failure of a community ownership trust in any way signal that other such trusts are necessarily heading for the rocks. After all, if the record of private land ownership in the Highlands and Islands was to be judged by the number of landlords who have gone spectacularly bust, often with very bad consequences for their tenants and dependants, then time would have been called on such ownership very many years ago.

For the moment, of course, failure in the community land ownership sector in the Highlands and Islands remains hypothetical. So far, community ownership trusts have done well. So far, they have been a highly effective means of securing a wide range of public policy objectives. This is not to say that other varieties of landowner – government agencies, lairds of the traditional sort, organisations like the National

Trust for Scotland (NTS) or the Royal Society for the Protection of Birds (RSPB) – are incapable of contributing to Highlands and Islands betterment. In one key respect, however, community ownership trusts are always likely to perform better from a public policy perspective than owners of the type still prevalent in much of the Highlands and Islands. Many individual landlords, all official agencies and all environmentalist bodies like NTS and the RSPB (a number of which have bought into the Highlands and Islands in recent years) manage their land in accordance with objectives laid down at a distance, and mostly they do so in a manner that gives people living on the land thus managed no say in what is, or should be, done with it. Even when some say is provided, it is always on a consultative basis – ultimate control resting with a particular property's owner, not its occupants. Lacking control, the residents of such an estate are never going to have their self-confidence and self-esteem boosted in the striking way that self-confidence and self-esteem have been boosted by the experience of community ownership – this experience bringing responsibilities, and opening up opportunities, otherwise not to be got. That is why governments in Edinburgh and London – if these governments are as serious as they say they are about promoting enterprise and self-reliance – should be doing more than they are doing presently to aid community land ownership's expansion.

Today, to repeat, you can stand on any one of more than 500,000 acres in the Highlands and Islands and, on asking some local person who owns that acre, get the answer, 'Us.' In years to come, this question needs to produce that same response when it is posed not on any one of 500,000 acres but on any one of millions.

Sources and bibliography

As mentioned in its Acknowledgements section, this book depends heavily on interviews and conversations with people involved in the community ownership trusts mentioned in my text. Most of these interviews took place on location, as it were, but a handful were conducted by telephone. Visits to localities in community ownership were also hugely helpful in that they provided opportunities to see something at first hand of the community ownership movement's many achievements.

Community ownership trusts also made available to me their business plans and other documents of that kind. A number of these are in any case available on trust websites – some of which are more comprehensive than others but all of which are valuable sources of information.

Because I have had some involvement in the community ownership movement since the 1980s, I had, prior to starting work on this book, a working knowledge of the movement's history. This was supplemented by extensive reading in newspaper archives. The principal newspapers and periodicals consulted were *The Herald*, *The Scotsman*, *The Crofter* (issued quarterly to members of the Scottish Crofting Federation) and the *West Highland Free Press*. The latter is very much the principal newspaper of record in a community ownership context. Every issue between January 1989 and September 2011 was examined.

————

There are books about the beginnings of one or two community ownership trusts. The most important are:

John MacAskill, *We Have Won the Land: The Story of the Purchase by the Assynt Crofters Trust of the North Lochinver Estate*, (Acair), Stornoway, 1999.

Janet Hunter, *A Future for North Harris: The North Harris Trust*, (North Harris Trust), Tarbert, 2007.

Any reader wishing to get some sense of the causes and consequences of the Highland Clearances, should start with:

Eric Richards, *The Highland Clearances*, (Birlinn), Edinburgh, 2008.

Organised campaigning for land reform in the Highlands and Islands began in the 1880s and continued into the 1920s. There are a number of studies of this period. By way of introduction consult:

James Hunter, *The Making of the Crofting Community*, (John Donald), Edinburgh, 1976.

Ewen A. Cameron, *Land for the People: The British Government and the Scottish Highlands, 1880–1925*, (Tuckwell Press), East Linton, 1996.

The most recent edition of the first of these books, published by Birlinn in 2010, contains a brief postscript on the development of the community ownership movement.

The oldest community ownership body in the Highlands and Islands is the Stornoway Trust which, as explained in Chapter Two, owes its existence to Lord Leverhulme. There are several accounts of his involvement with Lewis. An especially good one is:

Roger Hutchinson, *The Soap Man: Lewis, Harris and Lord Leverhulme*, (Birlinn), Edinburgh, 2003.

Key texts of the modern land reform movement in Scotland, which began in the 1960s and 1970s, are:

John McEwen, *Who Owns Scotland?*, (Edinburgh University Student Publications Board), Edinburgh, 1977.

John McGrath, *The Cheviot, the Stag and the Black, Black Oil*, (Eyre Methuen), London, 1981.

Andy Wightman, *Who Owns Scotland?*, (Canongate), Edinburgh, 1996.

Donald Dewar, *Land Reform for the Twenty-First Century: The 1998 McEwen Lecture*, (Friends of John McEwen), Perth, 1998.

Andy Wightman, *The Poor Had No Lawyers: Who Owns Scotland and How They Got It*, (Birlinn), Edinburgh, 2010.

Also important in this connection are the various reports of the Scottish Office's Land Reform Policy Group as published by the Scottish Office during 1998 and 1999.

There is beginning to be an academic literature dealing with community land ownership and related matters. The best starting point in this context is:

Charles R. Warren, *Managing Scotland's Environment*, (Edinburgh University Press), Edinburgh, 2009.

Among a growing number of relevant articles and reports are (in chronological order):

J. Bryden and K. Hart, 'Land Reform, Planning and People: An Issue of Stewardship?', in, George Holmes and Roger Crofts (eds), *Scotland's Environment: The Future*, (Tuckwell Press), East Linton, 2000.

D. C. MacMillan, 'An Economic Case for Land Reform', *Land Use Policy*, 17, 2000.

H. Chevenix-Trench and L. J. Philip, 'Community and Conservation Land Ownership in Highland Scotland', *Scottish Geographical Journal*, 117, 2001.

A. F. D. Mackenzie, 'On the Edge: "Community" and "Sustainability" on the Isle of Harris', *Scottish Geographical Journal*, 117, 2001.

I. MacPhail, 'Relating to Land: The Assynt Crofters Trust', *Ecos*, 23, 2002.

C. Warren, 'Occupying the Middle Ground: The Future of Social Ownership in Scotland', *Ecos*, 23, 2002.

J. MacAskill, 'The Community Right to Buy in the Land Reform (Scotland) Act 2003', *Scottish Affairs*, 49, 2004.

A. F. D. Mackenzie, J. MacAskill, G. Munro and E. Seki, 'Contesting Land, Creating Community, in the Highlands and Islands, Scotland', *Scottish Geographical Journal*, 120, 2004.

A. F. D. Mackenzie, ''S Leinn Fhèin am Fearann (The Land is Ours): Re-claiming Land, Re-creating Community, North Harris, Outer Hebrides', *Environment and Planning*, 24, 2006.

A. F. D. Mackenzie, 'A Working Land: Crofting Communities, Place and the Politics of the Possible in Post-Land Reform Scotland', *Transactions of the Institute of British Geographers*, 31, 2006.

J. Bryden and C. Geisler, 'Community-Based Land Reform: Lessons from Scotland', *Land Use Policy*, 24, 2007.

M. Aitken, B. Cairns and S. Thake, *Community Ownership and Management of Assets*, Joseph Rowntree Foundation, 2008.

M. Satsangi, 'Community Land Ownership, Housing and Sustainable Local Communities', *Planning Practice and Research*, 24, 2009.

C. R. Warren and R. V. Birnie, 'Repowering Scotland: Wind Farms and the "Energy or Environment?" Debate', *Scottish Geographical Journal*, 125, 2009.

A. F. D. Mackenzie, 'A Common Claim: Community Land Ownership in the Outer Hebrides', *International Journal of the Commons*, 4, 2010.

C. Macleod, T. Braunholtz-Speight, I. MacPhail, D. Flyn et al, *Post-Legislative Scrutiny of the the Land Reform Scotland Act: Final Report*, Rural Affairs and Environment Committee: Scottish Parliament, 2010.

A. Pillai, 'Sustainable Rural Communities: A Legal Perspective on the Community Right to Buy', *Land Use Policy*, 27, 2010.

N. Thompson and J. Atterton, 'Twenty-First Century Clientilism?: State and Community on the Isle of Rum, Scotland', *Sociologia Ruralis*, 50, 2010.

C. R. Warren and M. MacFadyen, 'Does Community Ownership Affect Public Attitudes to Wind Energy?: A Case-Study from South-West Scotland', *Land Use Policy*, 27, 2010.

T. Woodin, D. Crook and V. Carpenter, *Community and Mutual Ownership: A Historical Review*, Joseph Rowntree Foundation, 2010.

C. Macleod, 'Assessing the Land Reform Process', *West Highland Free Press*. 11 March 2011.

C. R. Warren and A. McKee, 'The Scottish Revolution?: Evaluating the Impacts of Post-Devolution Land Reform', *Scottish Geographical Journal*, 127, 2011.

Index

Abernethy, Ken 4
Abriachan 136–37
Aitken, Bill 138–39, 187
Alexander, Danny 180–81
Alexander, Wendy 123
Allan, Alasdair 189
Allan, Susan 2–5, 9, 135
Archers 14
Arkleton Trust 49–53
Ardagh, Jamie 93
Arnish 34
Ascherson, Neal 38
Askernish Golf Course 164
Assynt 54–66, 69–70, 74, 87–89, 91,
   105, 112, 126, 138, 156–57, 171,
   191
Attenborough, Richard 73

Baird, Duncan 129
Bangor-Jones, Malcolm 56
Bannatyne, Neil 4
Benbecula 47–48
Bhaltos 149
Big Society 5–7, 10–11
Blond, Philip 7–9
Board of Agriculture for Scotland 25,
   30, 37, 114
Booth, John 95–98
Borve and Annishader 66–70

Brasher, Chris 104–05
Brealey, Reg 103–04
Brocket, Lord 103, 140
Brown, Gordon 37–38, 40
Bryden, John 50
Bulmer, Jonathan 141–43, 146, 149
Bute 73–74

Clegg, Nick 7
Callaghan, James 40
Callander, Robin 110
Cameron, David (Harris) 146–48,
   158–59, 176
Cameron, David (prime minister) 5–7,
   9, 11, 177, 180
Campbell, David 128, 187
Campbell, Neil 76–77, 159
Carnegie UK Trust 15
Carr, Colin 85, 90
Carr, Marie 85, 90, 93
Chamberlayne-Macdonald, Nigel 103,
   107
Cleland, Liza 30
Coastal Communities Fund 180–81
Comhairle nan Eilean Siar 77, 141, 173
Community Land Scotland (CLS) 15–
   17, 19, 60, 158, 180–81, 189
Community Land Unit (CLU) 100–01,
   104–06, 109, 126, 128–29, 142–43

Congested Districts Board 25, 29–31,
   37, 48, 113
Conservative Party 7–8, 10, 25, 27,
   29, 40–42, 68, 138–39, 153, 180,
   187
Cormack, Joe 93
Cornwall 10–11
Crichton, Torcuil 86
Crofters Commission 69
Crofters (Scotland) Act, 1886 24, 32
Crofting Reform (Scotland) Act,
   1976 48, 50, 61–62, 68
Crofting Trust Advisory Service 69
Crown Estates Commission 181
Cuba 8
Cumbria 10–11, 177
Cumming, Jenna 17–18
Cunningham, Roseanna 76, 186–87

Department of Agriculture and
   Fisheries for Scotland (DAFS) 25,
   37, 41–42, 48–54, 57, 61, 75, 79,
   183
Dewar, Donald 110–12, 177
Eckhart, Marlin 90, 92, 104, 174
Eigg 79, 82–100, 104–05, 112, 119,
   123, 126, 128, 138, 154, 160, 171,
   174, 177, 182, 191
Eigg Electric 95–99

Farnham-Smith, Bernard 83
Ferguson, Ronald Munro 32
Foljambe, Michael 69
Forestry Commission 37, 41, 49, 70–72, 119, 137, 178–79
Forsyth, Michael 68–70, 72, 74–75, 91, 139, 152–53, 177, 179
Foxley, Michael 86–87, 89–90, 118, 173
Fraser, Simon 52–54, 58, 60, 62, 90, 93, 101, 126, 129, 131, 143, 146, 148, 185
Fyffe, Maggie 84–85, 88–92, 94–96, 126–27
Fyne Homes 133, 136

Galson 149–56, 184
Gigha 2–10, 13, 15, 35–36, 119, 122–36, 139–40, 143, 146, 148, 150, 158, 171–72, 177
Gigha Renewable Energy 134
Gilchrist, James 149
Gladstone, William 24–25
Glendale 29–32, 36, 54, 112
Gloucestershire 14
Graham-Campbell, Neil 65
Grogarry Lodge 162–63
Growing Community Assets (GCA) 162, 175, 178–79
Guardian 84–86, 92

Harris 15–17, 32–33, 46, 52, 74–79, 119–20, 140–49, 157–59, 179–80, 182

Harris Stalking Club 157
Hellinga, Johannes 141
Hepburn, Ian 72
Heritage Memorial Fund 92, 105, 128
Highland Clearances 23–24, 56–57, 63, 102–03, 112, 151–53
Highland Council 60, 86–87, 90, 93, 97, 104–07
Highland Fund 68
Highland Land League 23–24, 152
Highlands and Islands Development Board (HIDB) 27, 37, 83–84, 112
Highlands and Islands Enterprise (HIE) 59–61, 68–69, 77, 87–88, 91–92, 97, 100–01, 104–07, 112–19, 128–29, 136, 143, 147, 162, 167, 175–76, 178–80, 183
Hinchcliffe, Stephen 104
Hitler, Adolf 103
Holmes, Sandra 128–29, 142–43
Horlick, James 3, 123, 171
Hudswell 11, 13
Hutchison, John 93, 100, 107

Ireland 30

Jackson, Keith 114–17
Jackson, Rachael 114–19
Jacobite Rebellion 23
John Muir Trust 104–05, 146–47, 157

Kennedy, Charles 49

Keoldale 74
King, Charlie 105–06
Knoydart 71, 79, 101–10, 119, 126, 128, 133, 138, 146, 154, 160, 177

Labour Party 27–28, 37–38, 40, 48–49, 60, 100, 110–12, 123, 128, 137, 153, 177
Laggan 70–72, 74
Land Reform Policy Group 110–12, 128, 137, 153–54, 186
Land Reform (Scotland) Act, 2003 25, 136–40, 154–55, 161, 178, 184–87, 189
Land Settlement (Scotland) Act, 1919 25, 37
Leaver, Ian 95–97
Le Grand, Julian 7
Leverhulme, Lord 31–33, 35, 54, 140, 150
Lewis 17, 20, 31–36, 50–51, 57, 140, 149–56, 184–87
Lewis Wind Power 150–51, 154
Liberal Party 24–25
Liberal Democrat Party 7, 10, 49, 60, 125, 136–37, 180–81
Lochhead, Richard 189
Lomas, Barry 184
Lyon, George 125, 130, 140

MacAlister, Lorna 130
McBrearty, Helen 4

MacCaig, Norman 54, 156–57
McConnell, Jack 177
MacCrimmon, Anne 63–64
Macdonald, Calum 49, 70
Macdonald, John (Lewis) 151–53
Macdonald, John (Skye) 66, 68
Macdonald, Finlay J 75
McEwen, John 38, 40, 110–11
MacFarlane, Murdo 29
McGrath, John 28–29, 182
McIntosh, Alastair 87, 191
Maciver, Iain 33–36
MacKay, Calum 157
MacKenzie, John 57, 59–63
Mackintosh, Cameron 105
McLean, Hector 86, 88
McLeish, Henry 177
MacLeod, Lorne 126
MacMillan, Angus 159–61
MacRae, Allan 57–58, 60–63, 69, 89,
    171, 177
MacRae, Angus 48–50
McSporran, Willie 126–27, 130–32,
    146, 148, 172
MacSween, Iain 157
Martin, John 4–5, 9, 15, 17, 135
Maruma *See,* Eckhart, Marlin
Melness 69
Miller, Isla 105, 133
Miller, Rhona 105–06, 133
Ministry of Defence 160
Morrison, Alasdair 137, 140

Mugabe, Robert 138
Mull 72–74

National Trust for Scotland
    (NTS) 192–93
Nicoll, Ruaridh 92
Nicolson, Alaistar 66, 68
North of Scotland Hydro Electric
    Board 27

Orbost 112–19, 179–80, 183

Pairc 184–87
Panchaud, Gerald 141, 149
Peacock, Peter 59–61, 90–91
Plunkett Foundation 13–14
Potier, Malcolm 124, 150
Princess Royal 99–100
Prior, Cliff 9–10

Raasay 24, 41, 49–54, 58, 61, 74, 112,
    191
Rennie, Agnes 151–52, 156
ResPublica 7, 9
Rhodes, Philip 103–04
Richardson, Rory 70–72
Riddoch, Lesley 88, 96
Ritchie, Bill 44, 54, 57, 59, 61, 64
Robertson, Andrew 53
Robertson, Iain 59, 100
Robison, Kenny 125–27
Ross, David 59

Ross, Willie 27–28
Royal Society for the Protection of Birds
    (RSPB) 193
Rum 83, 170, 182–83
Runciman family 83, 123, 171
Russell, Michael 183

Salisbury, Lord 25, 27
Salmond, Alex 177, 182
Sanderson, Russell 47–49, 68, 74, 79,
    112, 139
Scalpay 17–19, 69
Scandinavian Property Services
    (SPS) 56, 61–62
Scarr-Hall, Ian 143–44, 146–47, 157,
    159, 182
Schellenberg, Keith 84–90, 92
Scottish and Southern Energy 184
Scottish Crofters Union (SCU) 47–54,
    57, 66
Scottish Executive *See,* Scottish
    government
Scottish government 8, 19, 73, 76–77,
    79, 119, 136–40, 153–54, 161, 177–
    87, 189, 193
Scottish Land Court 62
Scottish Land Fund (SLF) 127–30,
    132, 143, 162, 175, 178, 187, 189
Scottish National Party (SNP) 40, 77,
    137–39, 141, 177, 181–83, 186–87, 189
Scottish Natural Heritage 37, 175,
    182–83

Scottish Wildlife Trust 83, 89–90, 93

Sellar, Patrick 24

Sewel, John 111

Skerratt, Sarah 3, 16, 173, 177, 181

Skye 29–31, 49–54, 57–58, 61, 65–68, 74, 112–19, 179–80, 183, 191

Skye and Lochalsh Enterprise (SALE) 68, 112–19

Sopwith, Thomas 140

South Uist 159–67, 171, 184, 188

Soviet Union 8

Stewart, Rory 11, 13

Stornoway 32–36, 50, 54

Stornoway Trust 33–36, 41–42, 112, 149

Storrie, Hannah 4

Sunday Telegraph 133

Taylor, Fred 17–19, 69

Teale, Joe 133

Thatcher, Margaret 40

The Cheviot, the Stag and the Black, Black Oil 28, 36–37, 57, 182

Thomson, Norman 154–55

Titaghur 103–04

Transfer of Crofting Estates (Scotland) Act 74–75, 152–54, 179–80

Udny-Hamilton, Margaret 86

UnLtd 9–10

Vestey family 56, 58

Virani, Nazmudin 141

Wake, Hereward 140–41

Wallace, Jim 136–37

Watt, John 100–01, 104–05, 126, 129–30, 142–43

West Highland Free Press 38, 49, 52, 86, 100, 126, 128, 141

Williams, Angela 106–07, 109–10

Wilson, Brian 38, 40, 49, 65–66, 100–01, 111, 123, 128, 148–49

Wilson, Harold 40

Wilson, Iain 105–06

Wolfe, William 182

Yorkshire 11, 13, 84, 90

Zimbabwe 138